Power of Habit

Rewire Your Brain to Build Better Habits and Unlock Your Full Potential

By: Discover Press

ALL RIGHTS RESERVED

No part of this book may be reproduced, stored in a retrieval system, or transmitted in any form or by any means, electronic, mechanical, photocopying, recording, scanning, or otherwise, without the prior written permission of the publisher.

Limit of Liability/Disclaimer of Warranty: the publisher and the author make no representations or warranties with respect to the accuracy or completeness of the contents of this work and specifically disclaim all warranties, including without limitation warranties of fitness for a particular purpose. No warranty may be created or extended by sales or promotional materials. The advice and strategies contained herein may not be suitable for every situation. This work is sold with the understanding that the publisher is not engaged in rendering medical, legal, or other professional advice or services. If professional assistance is required, the services of a competent professional person should be sought. Neither the publisher nor the author shall be liable for damages arising therefrom. The fact that an individual, organization, or website is referred to in this work as a citation and/or potential source of further information does not mean that the author or the publisher endorses the information the individuals, organization, or website may provide or recommendations they/it may make. Further, readers should be aware that websites listed on this work may have changed or disappeared between when this work was written and when it is read.

Table of Contents

Introduction 4

Chapter 1: Why You Are Who You Are 6

Chapter 2: Making and Changing Habits 21

Chapter 3: How Habits Help You Get What You Want 37

Chapter 4: Foundation Habits—Mindset 48

Chapter 5: Micro-Habits, Massive Results 69

Chapter 6: Habits for a Better Life 90

Chapter 7: Big Habits 123

Chapter 8: Putting It All Together 132

Final Thoughts: Real People, Real Results 142

Introduction

"We are what we repeatedly do. Excellence, then, is not an act, but a habit." ~ Aristotle

Most of us have a habit (or two, or several) that we wish we didn't have. And most of us have a list of habits we wish we could adopt.

So, why don't we get rid of the bad habits and start building new habits today? Why do we procrastinate? Or, why do we start building a new habit and then quit the moment "life" gets in the way?

The mystery of habits seems to be one of the great paradoxes of being human. We *know* that habits are powerful, and yet, we are often powerless against the ones that take us in the opposite direction of our goals, and we are seemingly powerless in adopting the ones that could take us in the right direction.

In this book we will explore why habits are such powerful drivers of our lives and why they are so beneficial. We will also explore the nature of habits, why they are so easy to adopt and so hard to break, how habits are formed, and the theory on how to change them. After, we will dive into *why* changing habits is so hard (it's not what you think), and then a simple, straightforward, and extremely effective method of creating new habits.

As tempting as it may be to skip ahead to the juicy part where we talk about how to actually create habits, it's important to understand them first. Otherwise, bad habits will remain as well-established "programs" running in the background waiting to reassert themselves at the first sign of difficulty or even in a moment of inattention.

First, you will be introduced to simple-to-follow exercises that will prepare you for adopting a new habit. By the time you get to the "meat" of the book (the most powerful habits), you will understand why you are doing it this way, and you will be prepared to succeed. You will be empowered to make some amazing positive changes in important areas of life, and the skills you learn are transferable to absolutely anything you want to upgrade.

If you follow this method and faithfully do the exercises, you will see that within a month you can be enjoying at least one positive new habit.

Are you ready? Let's do this!

Chapter 1: Why You Are Who You Are

You Are the Sum of Your Habits

"Watch your thoughts, they become your words; watch your words, they become your actions; watch your actions, they become your habits; watch your habits, they become your character; watch your character, it becomes your destiny." ~ Lao Tzu

Nearly every philosopher throughout the history of humankind has agreed that you are *who* you are and *where* you are because of your habits.

You are happy or miserable because of your habits. You are overweight or fit because of your habits. You are wealthy or poor because of your habits. You are unsuccessful or successful because of your habits. Your home is tidy or messy because of your habits. Your car is well-maintained or a beater because of your habits. You have great relationships with people or not because of your habits.

Habits are like a program that runs constantly in the back of the mind, with the sole purpose of making your life easier (not "better," necessarily, just "easier").

In the next section, we will explore the science behind habits as a way to understand why they are beneficial (or rather, why they could be beneficial).

Habits are Awesome!

"Your beliefs become your thoughts, your thoughts become your words, your words become your actions, your actions become your habits, your habits become your values, your values become your destiny." ~ Gandhi

Habits simplify your life. They are your brain's way of automating behaviors that don't require a lot of complex thought so that you can devote your mental resources to the tasks that are more challenging. This is what I mean by making your life easier—you don't have to think as much when you are acting out of habit. Of course, that habit could be taking you in a direction you want to go, or not; but the point is, it's EASY.

Think about how you dry yourself off after a shower, how you get dressed, what you eat for breakfast, how you wash a plate in the sink, how you tie your shoes, the way you start and finish an email…every day, you do these things automatically without really thinking about them. You perform these actions in virtually the same way, in the same order, every time.

Now think about something you have just learned to do or are in the process of learning. Learning takes a lot of mental focus. While you are learning, you don't want to engage in conversation or do anything that pulls your attention away from mastering this task. Now, imagine how much mental effort you would have to expend on a daily basis doing something as simple as tying your shoes. Once upon a time, this task was difficult and required your concentration. Now, you can do it with your eyes closed (try it, if you don't believe me).

If you really think about it, your everyday experience is essentially the same because of your habits.

This means that a big part of your life is almost entirely on autopilot. Your financial status, your career success, your health, and your relationships all run to some extent on autopilot.

When you think about it in terms of efficiency, give your brain a big "high five" because of how masterfully it simplifies your life! It's truly amazing!

Every aspect of our lives is largely governed by habits, or behaviors that were mastered so well they have become automatic.

For example, most of us eat the same 36 items on a regular basis. Not because these food items are especially nutritious or delicious, but because we are familiar with them, we know how to prepare them, we know how they are going to make us feel.

In essence, you can equate "habit" with "ease."

It's much easier to follow along a well-trodden path than it is to forge a new path.

The irony is that even if the old path is unpleasant, it's familiar, and there's *something about it* that generates a reward.

This predictability of reward is what keeps us stuck in self-defeating habits. Intellectually we know they are moving us in the wrong direction, but they are just so rewarding.

However, a good habit can become just as easy as a bad habit, so there is hope!

This is a critical element of changing habits, so I encourage you to keep it in mind when you start replacing a habit you don't want with one that will move you in the right direction.

Consider the following quote:

"Sow a thought, and you reap an act; sow an act, and you reap a habit; sow a habit, and you reap a character; sow a character, and you reap a destiny." ~ Charles Reade

What this is really saying is that if you make a habit of something, that habit will make it *easy* to move in that direction.

Whether your habits are poor or rich, fit or fat, your habits make it *easy* to continue on that path indefinitely and achieve any goal you set your mind to.

Now, I know what you are thinking—*"There's no way it's going to be easy to achieve my goals!"*

Am I right? The truth is, the process may not be entirely easy, but a large portion of it will become easy simply because it has been automated. The less thinking you have to do about performing a task, the more likely you are to do it. You won't talk yourself out of it. You won't second-guess yourself. You won't worry about whether you can do it or whether you have time for it.

You just do it, repeatedly, and move a step at a time toward your best life.

We will get more in-depth into habits specific to each of these areas of life later in the book.

Habits Help You Achieve Goals

"First forget inspiration. Habit is more dependable. Habit will sustain you whether you are inspired or not....Habit is persistence in practice."
~ Octavia Butler

Setting a goal is often the logical first step in making a change. After all, you must know what you want before you go get it.

But why is achieving goals such a challenge? Why is it that millions of people make New Year's resolutions, only to break them within four weeks of starting?

The answer lies in that goals and habits are vastly different in the way your brain processes them emotionally. As you read through the following challenges with goals, think about the emotions that come up when you experience each aspect of goal-setting.

- Thinking about goals is exciting. Achieving goals is not.
- Goals rely on self-discipline and willpower.
- The process of achieving goals isn't always rewarding or inspiring.
- Goals are time-bound and they have an end point, and this often leads to frustration.
- Goals aren't guaranteed, and you know it, which can lead to self-sabotage.

Later in the book, we'll go in-depth into how to actually achieve your goals using habits, which are far, far more powerful than goals.

Habits Help You Have Better Relationships

"Life is habit. Or rather life is a succession of habits." ~ Samuel Beckett

There is a wonderful saying: "As I am with one thing, I am with everything."

If you have several unsupportive habits—for example, in health (you're addicted to junk food) and finances (you like shopping just a little too much)—there is a very good chance that you have unsupportive habits in relationships as well.

The way you behave around your partner, parents, children, siblings or anyone else is a habit. The way you react when they do something that upsets you, the way you ask them to do something—it's all habits. Families get into patterns with certain people behaving in certain ways and say, "That's the way they are."

Adopting new relationship habits can be more challenging because there is the other element (the other person), and you can't (shouldn't) change them. However, you will soon learn that you can develop habits that allow you to change your interpretation of what other people say and do, help you to choose a better response, and get out of the ruts that have become so easy and familiar—and so emotionally charged.

Adopting the right "people habits" can dramatically change all of your interpersonal relationships.

Habits Help You Become Successful (and Wealthy)

"Your net worth to the world is usually determined by what remains after your bad habits are subtracted from your good ones." ~ Benjamin Franklin

One of the most popular goals and New Year's resolutions is to become wealthy.

Assuming you have a number figure in mind (wealth means something quite different to everyone), what habits do you currently have that take you in the right direction? Write them down.

What habits do you currently have that take you in the wrong direction? Write them down. These are the ones you will be working on during the later chapters in this book.

Habits will not change your financial status overnight, but here's the thing about money: once you have some habits that support growing wealth, you can grow your portfolio exponentially with very little extra effort.

Habits Help Make You Healthier

"The doctor of the future will give no medicine, but will instruct his patients in care of the human frame, in diet, and in the cause and prevention of disease." ~ Thomas Edison

Have you ever wondered about the old saying, "An apple a day keeps the doctor away?" There's much truth to it. A daily habit of eating healthy, exercising, getting enough sleep, and stress management can add up to an exceptionally healthy lifestyle that makes you far less vulnerable to diseases than people who don't take care of themselves.

We'll get more in-depth into health habits later. For now, take heart. No matter how busy you are, no matter how hard it is to commit to hours-long exercise sessions, even 15 minutes of exercise every day—which is really a tiny amount of time that you can squeeze in—can make a big difference over time.

The 80/20 Rule

"80% of the results come from 20% of the causes. A few things are important; most are not." ~ Richard Koch

The Pareto Principle, more commonly known as the 80/20 rule, states that 80% of your results come from 20% of your actions. Therefore, 20% of your habits—your repeated daily actions—are responsible for 80% of your results.

Really let that sink in.

Just 20% of what you do on a day-to-day basis drives 80% of your results.

Just 20% is a lot easier to work on than 80%. What if you were to replace 20% of what you habitually do with empowering habits? You would experience massive changes in your life, and that is the whole premise of this book—to help you make big, sweeping changes one habit at a time.

You see, you don't have to change everything you do; just the key 20% that is holding you back.

The Takeaway: Habits Make You Who You Are

"Sometimes I get the feeling that we're just a bunch of habits. The gestures we repeat over and over, they are just our need to be recognized. Without them, we'd be unidentifiable. We have to reinvent ourselves every minute." ~ Nicole Krauss

Our habits define us. This is true for every single human being on this planet.

Goal achievement, greater wealth, better relationships, and better health all depend on creating better habits.

Imagine how different your life would be if you swapped out just a few of your bad habits and replaced them with good ones. Not all, remember—just 20% (the ones that matter most). Those are the ones we will tackle in this book. The smaller habits will be much easier to change, but you will get immense satisfaction from seeing fast results after changing a few of your big, bad, silly habits.

The following exercise will help illustrate just how quickly daily repetition of something incredibly awkward becomes fluid and easy, just like any habit. Do this one just for fun.

The Toothbrush Exercise

"Success is the sum of small efforts repeated day in and day out." ~ Robert Collier

Changing a habit is a lot like retraining conditioned muscle memory. Think about how every tiny movement involved with brushing your teeth is so incredibly well-rehearsed you could do it with your eyes closed, sitting or standing, even walking around the house. There's a very particular way you brush your teeth, every single day. You don't think about it, you just do it.

When you first learned to brush your teeth, you had to think about every movement. One way to quickly learn a new habit is to attach it to one you are already extremely good at. In this exercise, you will simply use your opposite hand to brush your teeth.

You'll enjoy this challenge, because there's no pressure. It's just pure fun and it's a huge confidence boost. For fun, take note of the date you begin the Toothbrush Exercise and when you master it.

Please read all the way through the exercise before starting.

For the next 30 days (or however long it takes until the movements feel completely natural and automatic), do your normal tooth-brushing sequence using your other hand.

The only rule is that this applies to every single part of the sequence from start to finish.

Sounds simple, right? It's actually very difficult in the beginning. But if you stick with it, within a few days you will see how quickly you are adapting. Partly, it's because you know what comes next; and partly, it's because you are so good at brushing your teeth your normal way that using your other hand doesn't seem too "out there" (impossible).

This process includes every single step:
- Pick up the toothpaste with your opposite hand.
- Unscrew the cap with your opposite hand.
- Pick up your toothbrush with your opposite hand.
- Squeeze the toothpaste onto the brush with your opposite hand.

- Brush your teeth as you normally do, but with your opposite hand.
- Clean your brush with your opposite hand.
- Replace the cap on the toothpaste tube with your opposite hand.

When you have to think about every tiny step, this thing you do every day is actually quite complex! It will feel strange for a while, but that's okay. A lot is happening in your brain as new neural pathways are created and you are learning new motor skills. It's really the same as when you first learned to brush your teeth!

Here are the rules to this exercise:

1. Take extra time to do this at first and do it slowly. Because of its complexity, this exercise is challenging and you will make lots of mistakes the first few times. You will need some time for your first few tries. You will have to *think* about each movement and how to perform it with your opposite hand before you actually do it!

2. If you make a mistake and do something with your usual hand, STOP. Replace everything and start the exercise from the beginning again.

Do this every day, each time you brush your teeth (you may need to start a few minutes earlier than normal, so you are not feeling stressed about having to rush to work).

After the first few days, the actions become easier and more fluid. Within a month, you will have created an entirely new habit of brushing your teeth. By this point, the entire process will take the same amount of time as your old tooth-brushing routine!

Repetition and consistency are the key! If you do this exercise daily until it becomes automatic, you will succeed.
But don't stop there. You have already used an existing habit as a jumping-off point. Continue with this and you will understand how changing a habit can radically change your life.

Once you have mastered brushing your teeth with your opposite hand, change the sequence of brushing—still using your opposite hand. If you always begin on the right side of your mouth, begin on the left side. It's amazing how many small, intricate movements go into the brushing process!

The final challenge is to use this new sequence of brushing with your original tooth-brushing hand.

Doing everything with your opposite hand is surprisingly awkward and difficult at first. Have a laugh about it. It's fun being a beginner! In the beginning it will take all your concentration to get it right. You really have to consider every movement, and at first your movements will be jerky and awkward, unlike the fluid and easy movements your dominant hand performs flawlessly.

What is really amazing about this exercise is how quickly you adapt. Each time you do the tooth-brushing sequence with your opposite hand, you are creating new thought patterns and learning new motor actions. Some movements may feel natural at first while others may remain awkward for weeks. But before the month is over, these become familiar and routine...and *easy*.

One day, you will be surprised to notice that you are naturally and easily brushing your teeth with your other hand, from beginning to end, *without thinking about it.* This is the point at which you know you have created a habit! You have completely automated the new movements to the point there is no need for conscious thought.

And by this time, you have also gained confidence. You are now an ambidextrous tooth-brusher, just as "fluent" in your left hand as in your right!

Congratulations!

This exercise beautifully illustrates how quickly habits form. Most of the habits you want to adopt will probably be much easier than this, but the process is the same: learning a new behavior and repeating it until it feels natural and normal.

I encourage you to take this same lighthearted attitude when you are working on adopting new habits. Do it in the spirit of fun. *Wouldn't it be amazing if...?*

In Chapter 2, we will go into the theory of habits, which will help you understand why they are so easy to form and so hard to break; as well as insights on how to bypass the "hard to break" mindset most of us have about habits.

Chapter 2: Making and Changing Habits

Understanding the Habit Loop and the Key to Change

Understanding how habits are formed is key to understanding how to create habits that serve your goals instead of sabotaging them.

How Habits Are Made

"A single footstep will not make a path on the earth, so a single thought will not make a pathway in the mind. To make a deep physical path, we walk again and again. To make a deep mental path, we must think over and over the kind of thoughts we wish to dominate our lives." ~ Henry David Thoreau

Behavioral scientists have several theories about how habits are made. One of these theories is centered around a three-step progression:

1. Reminder (the cue)

Something triggers the behavior. The trigger could be a memory, or it could be something you see, hear, smell, touch, taste, do, or feel.

Exercise: Choose a bad habit that you want to get rid of. What is the trigger for this habit?

2. Routine (the behavior)

The behavior that follows the trigger. Doing something one or two times doesn't make it a habit. The more you repeat a behavior that follows a specific cue, the faster and easier it becomes to repeat the behavior.

Exercise: What is the behavior (habit)?

3. Reward (the real reason a habit feels good)

Reward is the real reason you engage in a habit. Whatever you do that results in enjoyment or relieves distress, releases dopamine in your brain, which results in pleasurable feelings. And of course, who doesn't want to feel good?

The memory of this pleasurable sensation becomes closely associated with the cue and the behavior. So, when you are exposed to the cue again, you remember the reward and engage in the behavior. Think about some of the habits you have that you would like to break. What is the pleasure you associate with them?

Rewards come in two types: intrinsic and extrinsic. You can use either, or both, to create any habit. Often, extrinsic motivation gradually morphs into intrinsic motivation.

Extrinsic rewards: You are using the habit as a means to an end. You seek *rewards for your efforts*. Extrinsic rewards can include:
- Noticeable and measurable weight loss (downsizing to a new wardrobe can be a huge motivator) or an increase in wealth.
- Approval or recognition from others.
- A prize or award.

Extrinsic motivators are a great way to get enthusiastic and take action, but beware. Unless the reward is really meaningful to you, extrinsic rewards are not enough motivation when things get tougher.

Intrinsic motivation: Feeling good about what you are doing *(feeling good with the experience of the activity itself)*. This includes pleasure at seeing progress and how far you have come, the confidence that comes from overcoming challenges, the satisfaction of learning and mastering a new skill, the thrill of overcoming your fears, and the joy of knowing that you are actually moving toward a dream instead of just thinking about it.

It might sound simplistic to say that satisfaction can be a powerful reward, but it can be, and often more so than extrinsic motivators.

Intrinsic motivation means that the habit itself is enjoyable. For example, even if the habit involves exertion, you realize that it hurts to push your muscles, but it's a "good hurt" that leads to strength and endurance. Even if the habit involves fatigue, you feel it is a "good tired" and you can relax knowing you have accomplished something. Internal rewards are all about how you feel, not any prizes or praise you may receive.

Exercise: What is the reward for a negative habit you have? Could you feel the same way by adopting a positive habit?

The Habit Loop

"The chains of habit are too light to be felt until they are too heavy to be broken." ~ Samuel Johnson

Unless there is no trigger…unless there is no behavior…unless there is no reward…the cycle of a bad habit will continue indefinitely.

If you get rid of the trigger, you can break the cycle. But what if you can't get rid of the trigger?

If you recognize the trigger and avoid the behavior, you can eventually break the cycle, *but* you will be in for some serious resistance from your brain.

If you get rid of the reward, you can break the cycle. One woman I know was trying to break the habit of drinking Coca-Cola all day, every day. She researched how much sugar was in each can or bottle, and scooped up that much sugar into a bowl. The visual of how much sugar she was consuming every day was so repulsive to her, that this was all it took for her to stop her habit.

The key is that habits are all about ease. It always comes down to ease, because what is easy is pleasurable. Sure, difficult things (challenges) can be pleasurable too, but just think about how aggravated you would be on a daily basis if tying your shoes as you are trying to rush out the door was an arduous process that required a lot of thought. More than likely you'd switch to slip-on shoes, just to get rid of the hassle!

Therefore, if a habit is easy, then undoing the habit can mean making the habit inconvenient or difficult. We will get more in-depth into this shortly.

Challenge

"A nail is driven out by another nail; habit is overcome by habit." ~ Desiderius Erasmus

On a sheet of paper, write down how you *feel* when you engage in a bad habit (or habits) that you have. Write down the habit (the behavior) and the emotional reward.

The feelings (the reward) are likely different for each habit. You may feel relief. You may feel pleasure.

Next, write down how you feel *after* this initial euphoric feeling has passed, which it will in a short time. What comes afterward? Is it still relief? Or do you feel shame?

Knowing how you feel when you indulge in a bad habit—and by this, I mean the full experience of it, not just the initial reward—will serve you well when you start taking the steps to release the old bad habit and imprint a new one.

It's important that you hand-write this exercise rather than typing it on your computer. Writing engages a different part of the brain, and because you have to think carefully when you write (there is no delete button) you can gain deeper insights on things than if you do online journaling or writing.

Next, we will discuss why it is so challenging to release old habits and why they are so "sticky."

Why Habits Are Permanent (Unless You Consciously Change Them)

"Habit is a cable; we weave a thread each day, and at last we cannot break it." ~ Horace Mann

Once you have developed a habit, your brain changes physically and functionally to make that behavior easier (more efficient). In fact, within 30 days, it becomes easier to do the behavior than *not* do it.

Since your life is structured around habits your life trajectory will continue on its merry way, because once a habit is ingrained, it can last a lifetime. Unless, that is, you consciously change it.

Think about some of the habits you have had since childhood. Some people bite their fingernails. Some people have a little ritual they perform before a competition. Some people start their day with meditation, no matter what. Some people always brush their teeth first thing in the morning, while others wait until after breakfast. Some people always wash dishes after a meal, while others pile them in the sink.

Challenge

This week, try to become more aware of the things you do every day; more specifically, *how* you do them. This will help you to make a correlation between certain behaviors and certain life situations you are experiencing.

Again, keep in mind that habits are automatic and unconscious; we tend to think, "This is the way I am," when in reality, we're talking about habits!

Why Change Is Often Hard

Why Normal Habit Management Methods Often Fail

"Knowing is not enough, we must apply. Willing is not enough, we must do." ~ Johann Wolfgang von Goethe

We all "know" that we should adopt better habits, so why don't we? Most of the reasons come down to one thing: fear.

The Effects of Fear on Releasing Old Habits and Building New Habits

The first step to adopting a new habit is to believe that you can, and this is often not the case. For example, if you have poor lifestyle habits, it can be extremely difficult to believe that you can be as fit and lean as an elite athlete, even if that is your goal. If your money habits have caused you to always be worried about getting through the month to your next paycheck, you may believe that wealth isn't achievable for you, and you will resist adopting wealth-building habits.

You may fear failure, you may fear change, you may fear upheaval in your life, or you may fear that the process will be too difficult.

Let's explore the fears that could be holding you back (and keeping you stuck with bad habits you want to break).

Fear of Failure

"It is impossible to live without failing at something, unless you live so cautiously that you might as well not have lived at all – in which case, you fail by default." ~ J.K. Rowling

It's understandable that fear of failure can hold you back. We've all been there! It's one thing to try to break a small bad habit and adopt a different small habit, but most of us feel that taking on the bigger habits could be an exercise in frustration, especially if we've failed in the past.

For example, New Year's resolutions are one type of goal that requires adopting at least one new habit. There's no way to lose weight without making healthy eating and exercise your daily habits; there's no way to get that book written without adopting a habit of writing every day.

Since most people fail at keeping their New Year's resolutions, it comes as no surprise that a large percentage won't even start because they are afraid to fail. And those who do start will quit the moment something gets in the way. Of the 50% of adults in the United States who make New Year's resolutions, less than 10% keep them for more than a few months. Quitting is often related to difficulty when breaking old habits.

Fear of Change

"There is no life without change. The real tragedy is that we are always fearful of change and resist it vehemently." ~ Debasish Mridha

Change is inevitable, and yet, we hate it.

Whenever we're faced with an unknown outcome, the brain insists that we stay with what's known. From an evolutionary perspective, this makes sense. We stay in the valley where we know there is plenty to eat—even though there are enemies fighting for the same resources—rather than venture over a massive mountain range in search of something better. The change comes with great risk, and so the choice is made to stay.

Even though most of the habits we want to break or adopt are not life-threatening, that is not how the brain sees it. It simply sees that new equals uncertain, so the message is "forget it, the old is better, let's just stick with that." Through a combination of feelings as well as thoughts and mental images of what could go horribly wrong, your brain helpfully encourages you to stay in the safety of the known.

The fear of change can originate from your individual "risk appetite" or level of tolerance or aversion to risk. This can stem from childhood conditioning or your personal experiences.

For example, if you grew up with parents with a negative worldview—that the world is a dangerous and scary place—you would be less inclined to venture out of your comfort zone and try something new (even if it is for your highest good). You would be more likely to stick with what is known—including your bad habits—than someone whose parents shared their positive, adventurous worldview.

Change brings uncertainty, anxiety, rationalization of why you can't/shouldn't change, and avoidance. This resistance to new things is powerful! Fear of change is based on:

- Loss: Breaking a habit means losing something, namely the reward that habit brings. All the logical reasons we have for dropping a bad habit go out the window when emotion wins out. *"What if the new habit doesn't feel as good?"*

- Uncertainty: People would rather be unhappy than be uncertain, according to author Tim Ferris of the *4-Hour Workweek*. Breaking a habit means doing things differently for a while. It means breaking routines. It means doing something you are not good at. Science backs this up—the brain registers a new behavior (which has not been mastered) as a deviation, as an error, and compels you to go back to the old behavior, which is familiar and well-rehearsed. You start questioning it: *"What if I can't do it? What if it's uncomfortable? What if I look stupid?"*

- Lack of "why": Habits that you feel you "should" break are much harder to break than habits you *must* break because it is the only way to achieve the outcome you want. It's the difference between, *"I know I should make a habit of eating smaller portions, but I was brought up as a charter member of the 'clean plate club,'"* and , *"I am going to lose 20 pounds so I can look good at my wedding."* If your "why" isn't strong, you will find overcoming the fear of change to be a monumental challenge.

- More work: We all know that adopting new habits and breaking old ones takes work. *"But who wants more work? As if I don't already have enough on my plate!"*

Anytime something is rooted in fear, we become extraordinarily good at talking ourselves out of it. We rationalize why we can't and satisfy ourselves with the "wise decision" of sticking with what we know.

Why Willpower Doesn't Work

Willpower is not the most effective way to drop a bad habit and adopt a new one. We will go more in-depth into this topic later in the book; for now, it's important to know that willpower is a force that will be in a constant battle with your fears. In any internal battle, emotions almost always triumph over logic.

You may have a dozen reasons why you should drop a habit, but making yourself abstain takes extraordinary *ongoing* effort…and the battle will rage on and on.

The Myth of the 21-Day Habit

"Practice isn't the thing you do once you're good. It's the thing you do that makes you good." ~ Malcolm Gladwell

"21 days to a new habit!" You may have heard this from multiple sources, and in some cases, yes, you may be able to establish a new habit in 21 days. However, in most cases it will be more—anywhere from 30 to 90 days depending on how much internal resistance you have to the habit (or, how firmly the bad habit you're trying to replace is established).

We all know that we start to believe anything that is repeated enough times, whether true or not. So, we think, "Okay, I'll just practice a new habit for three weeks straight and it will become established."

This is rarely the case.

The 21-day myth dates back to the late 1950s. A plastic surgeon named Maxwell Maltz noticed that his patients got used to their new faces around the 21-day mark. Amputees would stop having phantom limb symptoms around 21 days.

He concluded that a minimum of 21 days was how long it took for an old mental image to dissolve and a new one to implant.

However, something was lost in translation over the years as people forgot the word "minimum." The belief was established that forming a new habit took 21 days, period.

Today, researchers, including Phillippa Lally of University College London, are finding that 21 days to a new habit is not the case at all. Lally's team studied 96 people over a 12-week (90 day) period and analyzed how long each person took to go from starting a new behavior to the point at which the new behavior became automatic.

The results of this study throw the 21-day myth out. On *average*, study subjects required more than 2 months (66 days, to be exact) to automate a new behavior. The *range* was surprisingly broad: anywhere from 21 days to 8 months.

Why? Because habits are rarely stand-alone. They are part of a web of habits that are unique to you. A change in one habit will influence others, but it will also be challenged by those established habits.

It's important that you do not put a timeline on forming new habits. Just let the process be what it is.

- Relax. Have some fun with it. Embrace the awkwardness (sure, laugh at the absurdity of how wonderfully you do certain things and how awkwardly you are doing this!). Congratulate yourself on the days when you do well and give yourself a break on days you struggle. Every step and misstep are important in creating new neural pathways that will eventually automate the behavior.

- Forget about time. Enjoy the process. As much as you want to get to the finish, relax and let the process unfold. Just as you watch a garden grow from seeds into flowers with gorgeous blossoms, watch yourself blossom into a person whose new habits have made a tremendous difference.

- Be consistent. You may have heard the 10,000 hours rule about fully mastering a craft. It's true that it does take ten years of consistent practice to become a master at something. But, you can speed things up with the quality of your practice, and not rely on just the quantity. In other words, "deliberate practice" is more important than showing up and going through the motions. Putting in the time alone will not necessarily make you a master. Quality practice means slowing down, being mindful, always doing your best, and relaxing into the process of learning, which includes making mistakes and failing.

- Mental rehearsal is proven to be essential to mastering any skill. The faster you can make something real in your mind, the faster you will live this ideal in your physical reality.

Whenever you practice a new habit, add mental rehearsal to it. Before and after doing this new habit, visualize yourself as already a virtuoso, a true master, in whatever you are doing.

The Secret to Breaking a Bad Habit: Friction

"If you pick the right small behavior and sequence it right, then you won't have to motivate yourself to have it grow. It will just happen naturally, like a good seed planted in a good spot." ~ BJ Fogg

Some people will take the approach of replacing a bad habit with a good one. However, this can be difficult because you're dealing with twice the resistance: resistance to breaking a pleasurable habit and resistance to doing something new.

Therefore, this approach requires a lot of discipline, which isn't always there.

You can do it, though, if you add friction to bad habits and reduce friction from good habits.

Breaking bad habits involves creating friction, or making it more difficult and inconvenient to indulge in the habit. For example, keep your junk food locked in your car.

Of course, the opposite is also true. The easier you can make it to do something positive, the more likely you are to do it. Remove as many obstacles as you can when you decide to adopt a new habit. For example, lay your running clothes out so that you put them on as soon as you get up.

There are a lot of great real-life examples of how people broke bad habits and created good ones in the last chapter of this book.

The Takeaway

"Habits are safer than rules; you don't have to watch them. And you don't have to keep them either. They keep you." ~ Frank Hall Crane

Fear of failure and fear of change could completely derail your efforts to adopt new habits. But don't worry, there are ways to overcome these fears.

There is magic in action. When you are in action, you are focused on what you are doing, and you feel less fear. The trick is NOT to take massive action, but a series of tiny steps. Just knowing that you are moving forward is enough to gradually ease your fears, and in this way, adopting supportive habits becomes just as easy as holding on to unsupportive habits.

In the next chapter, we'll discuss the power of micro-habits and how you can make relatively big changes by taking one small step at a time.

Chapter 3: How Habits Help You Get What You Want

Habits Are Better Than Goals

"First forget inspiration. Habit is more dependable. Habit will sustain you whether you are inspired or not....Habit is persistence in practice."
~ Octavia Butler

Setting a goal is often the logical first step in making change. After all, you have to know what you want before you go get it.

But why is achieving goals such a challenge? Why is it that millions of people make New Year's resolutions, only to break them within four weeks of starting?

Partly, it's that goals are usually big- too big to achieve without a fairly substantial amount of consistent daily effort.

As well, goals and habits are vastly different in the way your brain processes them emotionally. As you read through the following challenges with goals, think about the emotions that come up when you experience each aspect of goal-setting. This is important because most of the decisions that humans make are made emotionally.

1. Achieving goals is not as wonderful as we want it to be.

In the excitement of thinking about a goal, we tend to romanticize the process. We tend to see achievement as a series of inspired actions; in other words, we imagine ourselves feeling motivated and then taking action knowing that the act of doing feels good.

Not only that, but what happens when we achieve a goal? There's a brief moment of elation, and then a huge letdown and we think, "Now what?"

But let's start at the beginning of the goal-setting process.

What emotions did you feel when you set your latest goal? At first, likely you felt excitement ("Yay, I'm going to achieve this thing and then I will feel ___"). When you are in the honeymoon phase and it's "go time," you put forth a massive effort that moves you somewhat toward your objective, even though the prize is still very, very far off.

This initial excitement was probably replaced very quickly with doubt. The bigger the goal, the more doubt. This doubt is what drives your decisions, such as decisions to procrastinate. Doubt leads to rationalizations about why you can't achieve something. Once the rationalizations start, that's the end. This is when people give up, especially because achieving goals is more like an endless trek—often tediously boring—rather than a sprint to the finish.

With most goals, there is little inspiration along the way, even less motivation, and often, a lot of procrastination thanks to ongoing doubt. Then, rationalizations pop up when the smallest thing gets in the way of yet another day "moving toward" a goal.

What emotions did you feel when you got into a routine of the necessary daily actions?

Within a short time—once the honeymoon is over and the real work begins—you get into a routine, but the thrill is gone and the goal isn't getting as much attention as it did in the beginning when it was fresh and exciting. The goal becomes a bit of a struggle because it takes so much willpower to just do the thing day after day.

Habits aren't exciting, but you do them anyway. You may not be enthusiastic about them, but they are automatic, and so you do them without any internal argument.

2. Goals rely on self-discipline and willpower.

"Discipline is choosing between what you want now and what you want most." ~ Abraham Lincoln

Goals mean you have to do things differently. They mean giving up what you want to do now for what you must do instead, so you can enjoy the rewards later. And this requires constant willpower.

However, willpower is not infinite. If other parts of your life require willpower, you may not have enough to go around. For example, a goal of achieving financial freedom could mean saving a regular amount each month, but if you have a habit of impulse shopping, you are going to have to exert willpower each time a cool ad pops into your news feed.

And what if you have another goal of losing weight, which requires portion control (and lots of willpower to stick to those small portions when you still feel hungry)? Do you have the willpower for both of these goals, and not just once, but *consistently, every day*?

Habits do not rely on self-discipline and willpower, at least if you start off with tiny habits and work up to the bigger ones.

3. The process of achieving goals isn't always rewarding.

Humans are pleasure-seeking organisms. We prefer to move toward whatever feels good. So, when your everyday goal's actions don't give you an immediate reward, you need even more willpower to make yourself do it—to talk yourself into it.

The more emotional effort you have to exert in making yourself do something, the less pleasurable it is, and the less willpower you have for other things. Ultimately this translates to thoughts of, "this isn't fun anymore," and who wants to do something that isn't fun?

Then, something gets in the way. An injury. An unexpected expense. The weather. You are tired. You "aren't feeling it" today. *Maybe working on this tomorrow would be better, when I have more time...*

What emotions did you feel when something got in the way?
You put the actions off. You know that the goal is slipping away, and you feel disappointed—even ashamed, maybe. But then to your surprise, you feel something unexpected: relief.

That's right—*relief.*

Relief is an emotion that destroys goals when you realize it's a relief to give up the effort.

You don't have to make yourself do it anymore. You have rationalized your way out of doing something. Now you don't have to struggle. You don't have to work on your self-discipline. You have a reason for quitting. Then, it feels good to say, "Well, it didn't work out this time."

Habits (positive habits) are rewarding in that they truly make your life easier, and you feel good because you are doing something positive for yourself instead of self-sabotaging.

4. Goals are time-bound and they have an end point.

Goals are typically time-bound. "I want to lose 20 pounds by summer." "I want to buy a home by next spring." "I want to finish this book in time for Christmas."

What emotions do you feel when you don't reach your goal by the target date?

Let's say you managed to get through the low-motivation period of daily action and you have achieved your goal. Now is not the time to let down your guard (which is what most people do). Unless new habits have taken over, achieving a goal is a temporary bump or boost.

People set a big goal like losing a certain amount of weight, and then once they've achieved the goal, they go back to their sedentary ways…unless daily exercise and healthy eating has become a habit. If they still have to force themselves to hit the gym or cut back on portions, they will often reward themselves with an indulgence, which triggers the old habits.

Or, they reach their goal of making a certain income, but retain their shopping habits and so there is actually no change in their financial stress level as their spending keeps up with their income.

Ultimately, if you achieve a goal and you are still using willpower and self-discipline to do what you need to do, once you achieve a goal there's a very good chance that no real, meaningful change will occur. You will just go back to the way things were.

What emotions do you feel when you find yourself reverting to your old habits once you've achieved a goal?

5. Goals aren't guaranteed, and you know it.

Sometimes, despite our best efforts, a goal isn't attainable.

You might get a job that takes more of your time, which derails your goal of writing a book. You might incur an unexpected expense like a hospital bill or a major auto repair, which derails your goal of buying a new home. You might get injured, which derails a fitness goal.

In other words, "life" tends to get in the way of goals. Sometimes the goals are just delayed for a period of time, while other times the goals are simply shelved for "someday" or forgotten altogether.

We all know this.

This is why, if you *know* that achieving a goal is a "maybe" no matter what you do, it's much easier to give up at the first sign of difficulty.

What emotions do you feel when forces beyond your control make it impossible to achieve a goal, either within your desired timeline or at all?

Habits are guaranteed. You *will* do the behavior (once it's established) because it feels good and you know that these habits will take you where you want to go, and beyond.

Habits, as you are about to see, aren't shiny and exciting, but they are extremely effective.

What if you automated most of the tasks that moved you in the right direction so that you did them whether you felt motivated or not…and did them for the sake of doing because the "doing" feels good, regardless of the outcome?

For example, what if you made it a habit to sit and write for 15 minutes every morning before you got out of bed and before the day got rolling? What if you made it a habit to go for a walk every evening after dinner? What if you made it a habit to spend a few minutes each week to manage your finances?

Why Habits are Better Than Goals

"You'll never change your life until you change something you do daily. The secret of your success is found in your daily routine." ~ John C. Maxwell

The difference between habits and goals is not semantic. Each requires different forms of action. For example:

- You set a goal to become fluent in another language. You could set a goal to achieve fluency in two years, or you could commit to 10 minutes of practice each day. The goal is pretty intimidating, isn't it? After all, who becomes fluent in two years? Well…the person who practices every day has a significantly greater chance of becoming fluent in another language than someone who simply sets the goal and then practices sporadically. Over the long term, your habit of practicing something every day—even for just 10 minutes—can easily transfer that habit to any skill you want to master.

- You set a goal to read through the huge pile of books sitting on your bedside table (the books you say you will read "when I have time"). You could set a goal of reading the entire stack in one year, or you could decide to always carry one book with you so that you can make slow but steady progress on your lunch hour or on the commuter train. Or, if you work from home, you could make it a habit to read for 15 minutes before you start your workday (that way, you are assured that you won't be too tired at the end of the day). Either way, you will be making more progress toward your goal than someone who simply sets the goal and reads "when they have time." Over time, a habit of carrying a book with you could help you learn skills and acquire knowledge that will accelerate your career goals (of course, this means reading relevant books, not fiction).

- You set a goal to spend more time with your family. This goal could involve planning to spend the weekends on shared activities, but as we all know, this has a way of not working out, especially if everyone has different interests and as kids want more independence from their parents. Instead, you could adopt a habit of having dinner together every evening, with a rule of no phones or other electronics and no TV in the background. Over time, this habit will mean stronger relationships, better communication skills, and a deeper understanding of the people in your life.

- You set a goal to lose a certain amount of weight by the summer. You could get a gym membership and sign up for classes, and this could be motivation enough for you—although if you look at New Year's resolutions around weight loss, you can see that the statistics say that most people stop going within 30 days. Or you could adopt a habit of taking a brisk walk after dinner, for 10–15 minutes. This alone will give you some results, and as you get used to it, you could increase your after-dinner walks to 30 minutes and make real progress. Over time, the habit of daily fitness will strengthen your body so that if you ever become injured or ill, your body will be stronger and you will recover faster.

- You set a goal to save a certain amount of money within a year for a large purchase (such as a down payment on a home). You could say to yourself, "I will save (x) each month," but this may not work unless you are disciplined with savings. Adopting a habit of automatically putting 10% of your paycheck into an untouchable savings account—before you even see it—means modest but steady growth of your savings. Thanks to banking automation, this is a habit you can set up so you don't even have to think about it (the money is automatically transferred to your savings account). But if you want to create an actual *habit* of saving money, you could get in the habit of writing yourself a check if you're old-school, or going through a ritual of depositing money into your savings account each payday. The ritual doesn't have to be anything fancy, just expressing gratitude and a brief visualization of what you will do with the money. When you make it meaningful to save money by having a strong "why," then you are more likely to stick with this habit. Over time, this habit pays off big in helping you build a financial cushion for emergencies and helping you live within your means.

What's most important here is that your habits transcend your goals. They stick with you and act like a compass, or even better, like a railroad track that takes you to a specific destination and beyond.

Habits help you automate goals. The first step is setting a tangible goal. The next step is creating habits that make it, quite literally, a "no-brainer." And the final step—once you've achieved a goal—is to use those habits to transcend the goal and keep moving just as steadily toward a bigger, better goal.

Chapter 4: Foundation Habits—Mindset

Everything Starts In the Mind. Everything.

"Successful people aren't born that way. They become successful by establishing the habit of doing things unsuccessful people don't like to do."
~ William Makepeace Thackeray

This chapter contains habits that some people may consider "woo-woo." If you are among the skeptical, remind yourself that whatever you want to achieve, you must first conceive in your mind.

You think about paying your bills before you pull out your checkbook. You think about enjoying a cup of coffee before you get up and make one. For this reason, one of the best ways to adopt positive habits is to start by adopting empowering *mental* habits. In other words, developing a positive attitude that will empower you to take on the habits that will make a real difference in your life.

Starting from within, with your mindset, is absolutely critical to success. This is because our mental habits are even less obvious than physical habits. We can *see* when we act on our physical habits, but we aren't as aware of our mental habits. We think, "This is the way I am."

Every thought you have causes a physical reaction or

...us mind, where ..." Any repeated ... Every time you ... emotions.

... with things you ... at an ex-lover, that ... ry time you think ... nal reaction. This ... ey, your health, or

... drives your choices. ... are so effective. They ... t you to feel that your ... uy this thing or that

... control of your mental habits—and th... ... tional reactions—you can get control of your actions and, as a consequence, your results.

Habit: Prime for Success

"If you spend too much time thinking about a thing, you'll never get it done. Make at least one definite move daily toward your goal." ~ Bruce Lee

One wonderful habit to adopt is the habit of priming yourself for success every morning.

Do this first thing in the morning, when you have the opportunity to set the tone for the day. Before you start applying this habit, however, you have to know what your *ideal* day looks like and, more importantly, *feels* like. Whatever lies ahead for that particular day, take a minute to visualize (and feel) how you want it to go. During that minute:
1. Express gratitude for the day, and whatever it brings
2. Mentally rehearse *what can go right*
3. Mentally rehearse yourself feeling happy and confident
4. Mentally rehearse yourself easily and gracefully overcoming all challenges

Gratitude is vital. When you are grateful for what you have and the situation you are in, you have an emotional advantage over someone who is constantly wishing that things could be different or someone who is focused on what's missing. You are more resilient and calmer in the face of adversity.

If you spend just one minute on this habit every day, you will prime yourself to experience a better day. You will have a better attitude toward everything and you will be less upset by problems. Even if things go wrong, you will have an attitude of cheerful confidence, which will help you cope with practically anything!

Habit: Change is Easy

"If you believe you can change—if you make it a habit—the change becomes real." ~ Charles Duhigg

Change is hard because change is different. Right? As you have discovered in the previous chapters, change doesn't have to be hard at all. In fact, it can be just as simple and effortless as a series of micro-habits.

Adopting the belief that change is fun is a great habit to imprint. And yes, it's a micro-habit.

Change is only hard if you believe it's hard.

And who said change has to be hard?

There is no difficulty, no struggle, when the night gives way to the day. There is no struggle when the seasons change and leaves fall. There is no stress when a tomato ripens.

Life IS change. Change IS life.

So, forget about those big, sweeping changes. Do it in micro-steps. Every time you learn something, your brain physically changes. Every step you take is one step closer.

A lot of changes happen slowly over time, like kids growing up, and one day we wonder how they got so big. Each of us changes every single day. We may not notice, because the changes are small.

It's okay to make deliberate changes slowly too by building habits. Once you have one or several positive habits in place, you are firmly on the track to what you want. And it's easy.

Are you open to the idea that change is easy and fun? Are you open to the fact that it is what it is, and only *you* decide whether it is difficult or easy?

Every day, remind yourself, "Change is fun." Go ahead and repeat that tiny affirmation as often throughout the day as you remember to, and especially when you are thinking about changes you need or want to make.

See yourself with the goal achieved and think about how fun it *was* to get where you are now (in your imagination).

This is mental rehearsal for a brighter future. You have to imagine it before you can create it. And when you use micro-habits and bigger habits, it will be fun.

The Affirmations Habit (or, How to Stop Worrying)

"Worry is a thin stream of fear trickling through the mind. If encouraged, it cuts a channel into which all other thoughts are drained." ~ Arthur Somers Roche

Affirmations are phrases that you use to describe what you believe is reality.

Affirmations often become a self-fulfilling prophecy!

Remember the quote by Aristotle about excellence being a habit? He didn't just mean habits like avoiding snacking while trying to lose weight—he was primarily referring to mental habits and most notably, how you habitually talk to yourself.

Getting control of your self-talk through repetition of positive and empowering statements is one of the key secrets to a happy, fulfilled, successful, healthy, and wealthy life.

Going back to the 80/20 rule, 20% of what you say to yourself drives 80% of your decisions. This sounds silly, but when you recognize that a lot of the interpretations you make about events or the beliefs you repeat about yourself are habits, you can see that when you let this largely automatic and unconscious narrative run your life, your results will naturally follow.

How does self-talk guide everything you do, including every decision you make?

All day long, there is an internal monologue going on in the mind. What you say to yourself directly influences the results you get in life. You can talk yourself into, or out of, anything. You can rationalize why you didn't take action. You can tell yourself you are not good enough. You can repeat, over and over and over again, that there are no opportunities for you.

Many people will insist that they don't engage in any self-talk, but we all do. If you don't believe me, think about a subject you are worried about. Right away, your mind starts analyzing the situation through words and emotions.

What do you say to yourself when you worry?

Do you just imagine a worst-case scenario in mental pictures or feelings, *or do you talk to yourself about the problem you are facing and the potential outcome?*

Humans process things with words whether we are aware of this inner monologue or not. The trouble is that words feed feelings and feelings feed words, which influences your mood and your behaviors, which can reinforce the current situation and solidifies your interpretation of it.

Whether or not your interpretation is actually true is irrelevant. Every time you add a verbal description to a feeling or an image, you affirm, *"This is how things are."*

Think about the stories you tell people. You use the same words every time out of habit. It's exactly the same, and I do mean exactly, with the stories you tell yourself. Whether the stories you tell yourself are empowering or not is irrelevant. The point is you do it.

Whatever you tell yourself, you are already saying affirmations all the time! If you say, "I don't believe in affirmations," then you just used an affirmation!

The more you repeat an affirmation ("this is how things are") the more firmly entrenched it becomes in your mind until it becomes part of your reality—for better or for worse, because affirmations can support you or hold you back.

Negative affirmations such as "I'm not good enough" relieve you of the effort of even trying. But soon, you start to feel bad about yourself because the relief you feel is actually moving you in the wrong direction. And then you start to feel shame.

Cultivating a Habit of Positive Affirmations

"It's not what we say out loud that really determines our lives. It's what we whisper to ourselves that has the most power." ~ Robert Kyosaki

Cultivating a daily habit of saying positive affirmations can radically change your life. In essence, you are changing the automatic self-talk from being skewed toward the negative, to being supportive, optimistic, and empowering.

Retraining yourself to focus on the positive takes work. But adopting just one affirmation and repeating it consistently for 30 to 60 days will imprint the idea in your subconscious mind.

Why 30 to 60 days? You may have read that it takes 21 days to form a habit. That may be for some people and some affirmations. But if you are dealing with a novel idea that goes completely against your conditioned beliefs about how things are, it will take longer.

Expect to repeat an affirmation until you feel absolutely no resistance to it. Only then will you be ready to begin the process of imprinting another empowering belief.

Remember: Be sure to do just one affirmation at a time. The easier you make this, the more effective it will be.

Start with your biggest challenge area. Once you are in the habit of saying one affirmation and it "sticks," it will influence your mindset in that area of life, and you may find that that affirmation trickles over to influence your mindset in other areas of life.

Read through these success tips so you understand how to use affirmations effectively, should you wish to create your own. Then, choose ONE affirmation at a time related to your biggest challenge area.

1. Activate the placebo effect. Begin an affirmation session with "I am open to believing that this statement is true and right for me."

2. Take one minute each day to repeat one affirmation.

3. Repeat your affirmation as your daily mantra until you feel the statement is true for you, when you feel no resistance *at all* when you say the affirmation. Once an idea is firmly imprinted—to the point that it has started to become part of your normal self-talk—then you will be ready for the next affirmation.

4. Say your affirmations out loud if possible. This helps to keep you focused on what you are saying.

5. Write your affirmations on paper, in your best handwriting, as part of your 1-minute journaling.

6. Repeat your affirmation for as long as you can maintain focused attention on the subject (before your mind starts wandering).

7. As you repeat the affirmation, "feel it real." In other words, allow yourself to feel how you would feel if the situation or desired state of being were already real.

8. Stay focused and emotionally engaged. If you are saying something that currently isn't true, your mind will argue with it. That's why I recommend saying an affirmation when you are in a relaxed and happy state, preferably first thing in the morning before your mind starts chattering and you start to think about the challenges of the day.

9. You will get *some* results if you repeat your affirmations without thinking about them (as if they were background noise), but focusing your emotional energy on them fully is important to imprint in your mind that this is important to you.

10. It's easy to get into a trance-like state when you say affirmations over and over again, which is great because then you are in a relaxed and receptive state that makes it easier for the mind to accept the idea. This is why it's important to stick to just ONE affirmation. If you are trying to remember several affirmations, you will need to remain in an alert state *in which logic and reason can easily interfere and start arguing with the idea.* You don't want to give your mind the opportunity to argue, so a short, easy to remember

affirmation, repeated until you get into a relaxed trance-like state, is more effective than having to remember multiple statements.

Read through the list of affirmations below and choose one affirmation from a category that relates to the biggest challenge you are experiencing in your life.

Health
1. I love the way I feel when I take good care of myself.
2. Thank you for my health.
3. I create excellent health with good choices.
4. Every cell in my body is healthy.
5. I love and appreciate my body.
6. It feels so good to move my body!
7. I treat myself with love and respect.
8. I am grateful for strong, healthy cells.
9. I am willing to believe that my mind is the greatest healer.
10. I declare that I am in perfect health.
11. I practice excellent self-care.
12. I will sleep soundly tonight.
13. Every cell in my body radiates perfect health and vitality.
14. Happiness gives me energy and stamina.
15. Every cell in my body is healthy and happy.
16. I know when it's time to rest and when it's time to move.
17. I am filled with exuberant energy!
18. I feel attractive and energetic.
19. My body is functioning perfectly.
20. I enjoy a good night's sleep every night.

21. Health is my greatest treasure.
22. I make excellent lifestyle choices.
23. I look fabulous!
24. I drink plenty of water to stimulate my organs.
25. I enjoy a healthy diet.
26. I am grateful for physical strength and vitality.
27. I have the ability to positively influence my health.
28. I am strong and I am healthy.
29. I can do it!
30. I love taking great care of myself.
31. My energy and vitality are increasing every day.
32. I am open to the natural flow of well-being.

Happiness
1. I choose to be happy.
2. I choose to see the positives in every situation.
3. I am unstoppable!
4. It has worked, it is working, and it will work.
5. It's new. It's exciting. It's fun!
6. I am thoughtful, kind, and compassionate.
7. Change is exciting!
8. I am resilient and adaptable.
9. I choose to see opportunities in every situation.
10. I choose to see abundance and joy.
11. I choose happy, empowering thoughts.
12. I appreciate what life has given me.
13. I am free and peaceful.
14. I enjoy every moment.
15. I give myself permission to be me!
16. I appreciate what I have created.
17. I appreciate sorrow for it helps me understand joy.
18. My mind is focused on YES.

19. Did you know you are amazing?
20. I pay attention to what can go right.
21. You can do this, (YOUR NAME)!
22. I have a positive attitude about everything.
23. I am happy and grateful right now.
24. I am grateful for every part of my life.
25. I appreciate anger for it helps me understand compassion.
26. I choose to see the best in people.
27. I seek out experiences and people that make me feel good.
28. I appreciate this moment.
29. It's easy to cultivate positive habits!
30. I create the change I want!
31. I embrace uncertainty with playful spirit.

Wealth
1. I have more than enough.
2. I am grateful for the abundance in my life.
3. Large sums of money come to me easily and frequently.
4. I have more than enough money to meet every need and desire.
5. I am willing to believe that money comes easily to me.
6. I create wealth through my thoughts, emotions, and actions.
7. I declare that I am wealthy and prosperous.
8. My financial needs are being met in every way.
9. I can do great things with my money.
10. It is working out perfectly for me!
11. I feel abundantly wealthy every day.
12. Making money is good fun!

13. I hold myself to high standards of excellence.
14. Money is freedom.
15. I have high quality ideas.
16. I am grateful for abundance.
17. My skills and talents are money makers!
18. I creatively find new ways to increase my income.
19. I manage my time and my money very well.
20. I enjoy the circulation of money.
21. You have an open mind about new opportunities.
22. It's fun to explore innovative approaches.
23. I am raising my income ceiling now!
24. I enjoy and appreciate making (a number that is higher than your income ceiling).
25. My income is increasing every day.
26. I give freely and generously.
27. I appreciate the abundance I see everywhere.
28. I am open to the flow of great abundance.
29. I am relaxed. Everything I want is here, now!
30. I can make a difference with my money.
31. I always have more than enough of everything I need.
32. I allow abundance to come to me in surprising and joyful ways.
33. My talents and skills are important gifts I share with the world.
34. People appreciate my talents and skills, and reward me handsomely.

Success and Goals
1. I am a great success in everything I attempt.
2. I am a success every time I learn from mistakes and failures.
3. I have the ability to succeed.

4. I am grateful for this experience.
5. I imagine positive outcomes.
6. I am willing to believe that success is achievable.
7. I know I can overcome all challenges.
8. I achieve peak performance every day.
9. I am willing to believe that I can succeed at anything I try.
10. I have been, I am, and I will be successful.
11. My happiness leads to my success.
12. Success is inevitable for me!
13. Adversity makes me stronger and wiser!
14. My definition of success is perfect for me.
15. I feel successful.
16. I learn from successful people.
17. I am a peak performer.
18. I am great at getting things done.
19. I succeed masterfully.
20. I visualize and feel the joy of success.
21. Every "no" makes me better.
22. I have and use abundant resources.
23. Perseverance leads to success.
24. I can relax and have fun with this, no matter the outcome.
25. My habits support my goals.
26. I see opportunities and act on them immediately.
27. I make quick and excellent decisions.
28. If I can imagine it and believe it, I can achieve it.
29. It is possible for me!
30. Be bold. Be courageous.
31. I visualize the best outcome for me.
32. I can achieve my goals. I am achieving my goals.
33. I dream BIG!

34. There are many ways to achieve a goal.
35. I create success through my thoughts, emotions, and actions.
36. I am grateful for this opportunity.
37. I have many choices and options.
38. I cheerfully expect success.
39. I declare that I am successful.
40. I love taking inspired actions.
41. I believe in my ability to figure it out.
42. I am confident and capable.
43. I am ready! Go for it!
44. I can DO this!
45. Look how far I've come!
46. I choose to believe that I am capable.
47. I choose to believe that I am worthy.
48. I am willing to believe that I can achieve anything I desire.
49. I have what it takes to make my dreams come true.
50. I am confident and bold in my decisions.
51. As I help others get what they want, they help me get what I want.
52. Opportunities are everywhere, and I enjoy taking action on them.

Relationships
1. I am grateful for happy, healthy friendships.
2. I have an abundance of wonderful, close friends.
3. It is so easy to make good friends.
4. I have a loving, close relationship with my soulmate.
5. I am willing to believe that I deserve a great relationship.
6. I give and receive unconditional love every day.

7. My words and actions are expressions of love.
8. I remember why I love you.
9. I only speak words of kindness, integrity, and truth.
10. I am willing to believe that I deserve great friendships.
11. I create great friendships through loving kindness and compassion.
12. I declare that I have strong personal boundaries.
13. I allow my perfect partner to enter my life.
14. I am open to unconditional love.
15. All of my relationships are meaningful, happy, and fulfilling.
16. I am grateful for the people in my life.
17. As I love myself, I allow others to love me too.
18. I am open to love, in all the ways that love manifests itself.
19. I seek to understand alternative points of view.
20. I appreciate the importance of alternative points of view.
21. Forgiveness brings me peace.
22. Love is my language.
23. My positive attitude attracts the right people.
24. I appreciate and accept other people's perspectives.
25. I see the best in me.
26. I choose to see the best in others.
27. I honor my values by creating strong boundaries.
28. As I share my love with others, it comes back to me.
29. I appreciate my friends for who they are.
30. I am grateful for the opportunity to enrich the lives of others.
31. I freely give and receive unconditional love.

Purpose

1. I am living the life I am meant to live.
2. I am grateful that I know my purpose.
3. I have the courage to follow my heart.
4. I live passionately and purposefully.
5. I have the passion to follow through on my dream.
6. I matter.
7. I focus on what is meaningful to me.
8. It is my life, my path, and my choice.
9. I appreciate my creativity.
10. I am determined and focused.
11. I am enthusiastic and energized.
12. Thank you for my talents!
13. I am curious and playful.
14. I am in the right place, at the right time, doing the right thing.
15. I am focused on what can go right!
16. I belong. I am appreciated and valued.
17. I listen to my intuition.
18. I appreciate my inner wisdom.
19. I feel so alive!
20. I am excited about my future.
21. I love and accept myself.
22. I have unique and amazing talents.
23. I have a beginner's mind: I am teachable.
24. I love what I do and do what I love.
25. I'm in it for the right reasons.
26. I love the journey.
27. I will always do my best!
28. I am worthy of living a life of purpose and passion.
29. I have the means to fulfill my purpose.
30. I deserve to share my talents.
31. I honor my talents and gifts by developing and sharing

them.
32. I appreciate my talents.
33. I appreciate that I am unique and important.
34. I am grateful for my talents.

Mental Power and Creativity
1. I trust my inner wisdom completely.
2. I create desirable circumstances with my thoughts, emotions, and actions.
3. I am grateful for my creative powers.
4. My memory is amazing.
5. My mind is powerful.
6. I declare that I am a powerful creator.
7. I easily solve all of my problems.
8. I am grateful for the ability to focus on the solution.
9. I am open to alternative approaches.
10. I declare that I already possess the answer to any question.
11. I declare that I already possess the solution to any problem.
12. My solutions are creative and brilliant.
13. I always ask the right questions.
14. I listen openly.
15. What if it works out even better than I expected?
16. I wonder what inspiration will come to me today?
17. I trust my intuition to guide me in solving all problems.
18. I believe in my ability to solve all of my problems.
19. I am able to see the benefits inherent in all problems.
20. I learn from my mistakes and failures.
21. I appreciate my problems for their valuable guidance.
22. I am grateful for the ability to silence my thoughts so I can hear answers.

23. I experience inner peace and creativity as my mind becomes still.

Self-Love
1. I love myself.
2. I appreciate myself for who I am.
3. I am grateful for being a unique, wonderful, magnificent me!
4. I have an important purpose.
5. I have the courage to express myself.
6. My confidence is growing every day!
7. I am willing to believe that I am important.
8. I am willing to believe that I matter.
9. I am worthy of everything that I consider good.
10. I am worthy of having my every need met.
11. I honor myself by seeing myself in a loving light.
12. I am focused on my positive attributes.
13. When I see flaws in others, I recognize them as opportunities to improve myself.
14. I speak kindly, respectfully, and lovingly to and about myself.
15. When I see flaws in myself, I recognize them as opportunities to improve.
16. I forgive myself for my mistakes.
17. I demonstrate self-love by courageously being myself.
18. I give and receive unconditional love.
19. I love and accept myself unconditionally.
20. I am my own best friend.

This process of repeating affirmations works to create new thought habits, but you do need to be consistent with it, until an idea feels natural. Resist the urge to say more than one affirmation at this stage. Introducing too many affirmations at once can lead to feeling overwhelmed and internal resistance.

So, sneak one in there, and then another…and you will see that many of these affirmations won't even be necessary because you will already be in the mindset you desire to create. All it takes is one new belief in each area of life to influence positive changes in every area.

Once you are a "pro" at saying one affirmation and you are starting to see the results of your new mental habit, you can add just one affirmation to your daily routine. Eventually you could do up to three, but again, for the sake of being effective (getting into that relaxed trance-like state where you are open to new ideas), it's best to keep the number low.

This chapter has laid the foundation for creating positive habits. The next chapter outlines an astonishingly simple way to start adopting habits with practically zero effort. It is simply the easiest way you can go about making change in your life, in micro-increments.

Chapter 5: Micro-Habits, Massive Results

A Surprisingly Easy and Effective Approach

"I fear not the man who has practiced 10,000 kicks once, but I do fear the man who has practiced one kick 10,000 times." ~ Bruce Lee

When you set a big goal, even if it seems reasonable, you are going to run into resistance from your brain. Remember, it likes efficiency, it likes routine, and it likes safety. Stepping out of the routine makes you inefficient (the learning curve), and it is potentially dangerous (even if it isn't).

That's why even reasonable goals, like going for a 3-mile run a couple of times a week, are hard to achieve. As we discussed before, any kind of upheaval in your life—any change to your routine—is likely to end in failure.

Creating tiny habits is the secret to making positive change the easy way.

There is no struggle in adopting micro-habits. As you are about to see, this is the single most effective way to support major changes without going through "major changes."

Let's take the example of writing a book. In an ideal world, a habit of writing for just 15 minutes a day yields astonishing results thanks to consistency. Even though you don't always feel inspired, or sometimes what you write is absolutely dreadful, daily writing keeps the creative juices flowing while you make steady progress.

But—there's always a "but." Some days you come home from work and you are completely exhausted. Your son has a fever. You have been on the phone with tech support all day and the thought of spending even one more second in front of the computer is as appealing as having your teeth pulled.

If you have strong willpower and self-discipline, you can overcome these objections. But even one break in the routine often leads to resistance and rationalizations: *it's a great idea to write a book, "but maybe it's just not the right time…I'll start again when…"*

"When" never happens.

Why Micro-Habits Work

"Action is one, two is a coincidence, three of them forms a trend and suggests a pattern." ~ Thomas Vato

Enter micro-habits, or ridiculously tiny habits that cumulatively make a huge difference.

What would your life be like if you changed your trajectory by just one percent? One percent doesn't seem like much of a change, does it? At first, it is essentially the same as what you have been doing all along. But over time, that one percent difference is huge. If you drew a straight line that took you in Direction A, and then deviated from that line by just 1%, at first it would seem like you aren't doing anything to move toward Direction B; but the further you go, the more the two paths diverge, and soon it becomes clear that you have made a big change by doing something only slightly differently.

This chapter discusses several key micro-habits that will change your trajectory. This is your introduction to the power of small changes. You will be taken through every step in this chapter. In later chapters, you can apply this knowledge to making change in each area of your life.

What is a Micro-Habit?

"Habits stay with you even when you don't have the motivation." ~ Neeraj Agnihotri

A micro-habit is a small change in behavior. It's not "quit smoking" but rather, "smoke one less cigarette each day." Again, this can seem ridiculous and pointless, but as you are about to see, these tiny changes really do add up.

Micro-habits are something you can do in one minute or less, which makes them easy to squeeze into the busiest day, and, most importantly, makes them too small to fail.

Examples of DAILY micro-habits:
- Instead of trying to run three miles a few times a week, run for one minute every day.

- Wait one minute before reaching for a cigarette or drink.
- Make your bed every morning.
- Instead of cutting portions in half, drink one glass of water before a meal (it will make you feel fuller).
- Meditate for one minute.
- Drink one extra glass of water per day (your usual glass size).
- Do jumping jacks for one minute.
- Smile at yourself in the mirror for one minute (a game-changer as you will find out).
- Instead of starting your day with coffee, have a glass of water and then have your coffee.
- Wait one minute before automatically reaching for another helping of food.
- Do one push up.
- Do one sit up.
- Do one squat.
- Hug your partner for one minute.
- Put $1 (or some other "ridiculously small" amount of money, whatever that is for you) into untouchable savings *every day* (this could be a silly piggy-bank, so you don't have to go through the hassle of making an online deposit every day; you can transfer the money at your convenience to an interest-bearing account, just don't touch that piggy bank!).
- Take one minute to send a positive email or text to a friend.
- Practice one minute of gratitude as you drift off to sleep, or first thing after you wake up.
- Wait one minute before reaching for a sugary snack.
- Spend one minute tidying one small part of your home.

- Write in your journal or write down a few notes or thoughts for one minute.
- Add one fresh vegetable or fruit to each meal.
- Wake up one minute earlier, and during that one minute practice gratitude.
- Say one affirmation daily, as you smile at yourself in the mirror.
- For one minute, walk faster than you normally do.
- For one minute, stand tall (stomach in, chest out, shoulders back, eyes forward).
- Visualize your ideal life for one minute in the middle of the day.
- Use people's names at least once when speaking to them.
- Compliment someone every day (notice what people do, how they dress, etc., and show your appreciation; this teaches you to see the best in others).

The biggest benefit of these tiny micro-habits is that you will develop confidence, self-worth, and best of all, self-love. You are doing this for you! How awesome is that?

Quick question: which three of these micro-habits are you most likely to adopt if you could start today?

The point of micro-habits is that they are *easy*. Ridiculously easy, in fact. And, they are easy to add on to, both as spirit moves you (for example, on a day when your energy is particularly high or you aren't slammed with a lot of responsibilities), and more deliberately, over time.

Once you are doing one push up, you are likely to do a few more than that. But if you don't feel like it, just do one and walk away with the satisfaction of sticking to your new habit.

Once you are in the habit of doing one push up consistently every single day for as long as it takes the habit to "set" (typically around 30 days), then it's *easy* to add just one more push up to your daily routine until those two push-ups are a habit, at which point you add just one more.

Some of these habits are meant to increase over time. Others, like drinking water first thing in the morning and making your bed, are not.

How to Apply Micro-Habits to Your Daily Routine

"Your little choices become habits that affect the bigger decisions you make in life." ~ Elizabeth George

The Tortoise and the Hare

The classic children's fable, *The Tortoise and the Hare*, basically sums up the power of micro-habits.

> *A Hare was making fun of the Tortoise one day for being so slow.*
>
> *"Do you ever get anywhere?"* he asked with a mocking laugh.

"Yes," replied the Tortoise, "and I get there sooner than you think. I'll run you a race and prove it."

The Hare was much amused at the idea of running a race with the Tortoise, but for the fun of the thing he agreed. So, the Fox, who had consented to act as judge, marked the distance and started the runners off.

The Hare was soon far out of sight, and to make the Tortoise feel very deeply how ridiculous it was for him to try a race with a Hare, he lay down beside the course to take a nap until the Tortoise should catch up.

The Tortoise meanwhile kept going slowly but steadily, and, after a time, passed the place where the Hare was sleeping. But the Hare slept on very peacefully; and when at last he did wake up, the Tortoise was near the goal. The Hare now ran his swiftest, but he could not overtake the Tortoise in time.

The race is not always to the swift.

Likewise, when you adopt a few teeny tiny micro-habits, you will march steadily toward your goals, and you will be unbeatable.

Know Your "Why"

"The secret to permanently breaking any bad habit is to love something greater than the habit." ~ Bryant McGill

For any habit to succeed, including micro-habits, the habit has to be related to something you care about—some meaningful end goal—or you won't do even this small thing.

Your "why," or the real reason you want to do something, is not the thing itself. It is the feeling you get when you achieve a certain state. In other words, it is not the goal that you are after, it is the feeling that comes as a result of achieving the goal.

Here is an example of a "why" statement: "I exercise every day, I have a 32-inch waist, I have less than nine percent body fat, I'm full of abundant energy, I eat healthy foods and drink plenty of water."

Would you agree with that?

Actually, this is the *goal*. It is NOT the *why*. The *why* is something like this: "Exercise makes me feel attractive, confident, and energetic." How you got to this feeling state doesn't matter. This is the guidepost for your behaviors; not the specifics of the achievement, but rather how you will feel when you have accomplished it.

The Real Magic of Micro-Habits

"The less effort, the faster and more powerful you will be." ~ Bruce Lee

Individually, the significance of your new micro-habits is negligible.

The real magic is in your ability to create other new habits *quickly and painlessly*. For example, let's say you have a health goal, you want to lose a certain amount of weight, or be able to run a certain distance in a certain amount of time. It's not just one habit that will get you there (well, it could be, but the process will be much faster if you adopt a couple of complementary habits that are working together to move you toward your goal).

These new habits will, over time, build on themselves and help you achieve even the most ambitious goals that would otherwise be shelved because they feel overwhelming and impossible.

Remember: slow and steady wins the race because as you get "stronger" and "faster" you can increase the intensity and duration of what you do *automatically*.

Before starting on a few new daily micro-habits, make sure they align with your "why," or the *feeling* you want to have once you have achieved a goal. Always think of your big goals in terms of how you want to feel.

- You feel attractive when you put on one size smaller clothing and it fits.
- You feel confident when you achieve a personal best in a sport.
- You feel proud when you publish your blog.
- You feel relief when you achieve your financial goal.

Think about any goal you have now or have had in the past. It's not the goal itself that you are really after. Achieving a milestone gives you a temporary high, quickly followed by a kind of "now what?" feeling. What micro-habits do is make it easier to achieve a goal and then, help you keep going toward another goal—another carrot—that is even bigger and better.

The Process

Of that list of twenty micro-habits, you could simply add up how many minutes it would take to do them all (less than twenty minutes) and you might think, "I can do all of these every day, no problem!" Except, you won't. Twenty minutes basically equates to one big chunk of time that will get in the way of your routine. Plus, you would have to remember to do all these things, and that's just too much. It defeats the purpose of micro-habits.

Choose just five micro-habits from the list above (or substitute others that are more meaningful to you) with the only rule being that you do this thing every day, for one minute or less.

Wherever possible, do these habits before you get started on your daily routine. I know that this is not always realistic, but if you get up just five minutes earlier, you could achieve five things before anyone else in the household has opened their eyes, and with no disruption to your day. For example:
- Drink a glass of water
- Meditate for one minute
- Do one pushup
- Do one squat
- Smile at yourself in the mirror for one minute

Alternatively, if you are a night owl and do your best thinking and doing at night, then try doing your micro-habit routine just before bedtime. In general, most people are tired at the end of the day and therefore less likely to do this, but if it works for you, go for it. *That* you do it is more important than *when* you do it.

Once you figure out the time of day that you can consistently do your five minutes of micro-habits, stick to that time. Make it a part of your daily routine at a predictable time.

Micro-habits can't be excused away. They take so little time, and if you do these five things that are good for you before breakfast, you feel good because it is a wonderful way to start the day on a positive note!

The Reward

Micro-habits are a form of empowering confirmation. You said this thing was important to you, you said you would do it, *and you are doing it*, with no excuses.

Some people like to track their progress and if you are one of them, by all means do it. Make a checkmark on a calendar every time you perform a habit. If you are not a tracker, just do it. The key is to perform these micro-habits daily, no matter what. There are NO excuses in fitting five minutes' worth of habits into a 24-hour period.

The reward comes both daily, as you perform each habit, and over time, as you make slow but steady progress on your goals.

Success Tips

"Everything you are used to, once done long enough, starts to seem natural, even though it might not be." ~ Julien Smith

The whole process of adopting micro-habits can take just a few minutes a day—even just one minute, if you prefer to do one habit at a time! It's easy to break your self-work into bite-sized chunks that fit between appointments and tasks. If you have had trouble in the past with sticking with something new, start with just one micro-habit. Once you see how easy that is, you will be inspired to take on more.

Once any new behavior is a habit, you will see that it's as natural and easy as brushing your teeth. You won't argue with doing it—it will be an automatic behavior. And again, even though one micro-habit won't make a huge difference in and of itself, you can expand on that habit so that it has real results. You can also adopt a few other positive habits that will work in concert to move you toward your goals.

In this next section, we will explore a few micro-habits that will change your life in profound ways.

The Habit of Gratitude

"Drop by drop is the water pot filled." ~ Buddha

Many of us are in the habit of complaining. What does complaining actually do? Nothing productive. All it does is cause stress. Stress sucks the joy out of life. It makes you physically tired from being in a tense, red alert mode all day. It makes your thinking foggy. Being in a chronic state of stress, even if that stress is low-grade and you are used to it, can cause health problems. Reducing stress is key to a happy, healthy, and fulfilling life.

Replacing the habit of complaining with another habit—gratitude—helps completely change your perception of the world. You start to see the "silver linings" and the hidden benefits in adversity. You start to see the best in people. You become more appreciative of the little things you take for granted. You start to see that the world isn't against you, but rather that adversity is a valuable teacher. You start to see that most of the things you complain about are not even worth your time and energy.

The habit of gratitude is a foundational micro-habit. By changing your attitude, it fosters an abundance mindset that is necessary for achieving financial and career goals. By shifting your focus from what you don't have to what you do have, you become more relaxed and significantly happier because you are not in a constant state of wanting.

As a micro-habit, start with one minute every day. During that minute, express appreciation for:
- What you have
- The experiences and challenges that have brought you here to this point of awakening and personal growth

- ALL of the people in your life (including those who hurt, annoy, and challenge you)

At first, expressing gratitude for the "bad" things and people in your life can be difficult. However, the more you practice gratitude the more you will naturally start to uncover the reasons why unfortunate circumstances have made you stronger, wiser, and more compassionate.. You will start to uncover the reasons why annoying people are in your life. You will start to see that the choices you have made have resulted in certain outcomes, which is actually extremely empowering because if you could make those choices—and all choices have consequences—then you can likewise make better choices. You will start to see that each experience has taught you something (and if your most powerful lessons have been difficult ones, you are not alone).

If something pops into your mind that you feel you "should" feel grateful for—and you can't make yourself be thankful for it—think about at least one tiny thing that it did for you.

For example, a friend relates a story of a job she once had. She took the job out of necessity, knowing that the money was enough to keep her from losing her home to foreclosure, but also knowing that the job wasn't aligned with her interests. She soon found out that the situation was not a good one; the situation was toxic. Her boss was verbally abusive and frequently changed her mind about priorities and then berated her employees for not finishing a task that she had pulled them away from. The boss was a micromanager and constantly pointed out errors while overlooking the innovative ways that her employees solved problems. My friend only lasted one year before quitting.

Later, I asked her what she was grateful for, something good that had come out of that job. At first she said, "It helped me make enough money so I could refinance my mortgage and not lose the house." I encouraged her to dig deeper, past the financial benefits of the job. It took some time, but she finally came up with: "This job taught me how NOT to run a business and treat employees." She paused for a moment, and then it all came spilling out. As it turns out, the job had taught her a lot.

She said, "It taught me how to be a good leader and how to manage priorities. I learned how not to overreact to the smallest stupid 'emergency,' but to look at the big picture. I learned how to let people do their jobs, even if it's not the way I would do things. I learned the value of listening to people when they had an idea on how to do things more effectively or more efficiently. I learned a lot about a business I had never been interested in and I can transfer those skills to any industry…" She went on and on, listing more things that initially she had not been able to see in the stresses of the job.

Ultimately, the message was this: if you dig deep so that you can see even one tiny benefit in any adversity, you will uncover more and more to be grateful for.

In this way, gratitude will completely change everything. It will make you resilient, which is another necessary component of getting what you want out of life.

The path we choose is not always the one that will lead us to the destination we have imagined for ourselves. Gratitude helps us to appreciate the process, the journey, as much as we are grateful for the achievement.

The Habit of Smiling

"I will never understand all the good that a simple smile can accomplish."
~ Mother Teresa

Most of us don't smile enough every day. I'll let you in on a secret: If you smile more, you will feel happier. Smiling at yourself in the mirror for just one minute every morning helps you start the day with a flood of positive feel-good chemicals, and it is the easiest and fastest way to improve your life.

A friend tells the story of when her children were small. She said, "When my kids were in a bad mood, I would look them in the eye and say, 'I can make you smile!' They would angrily scrunch up their little faces and insist that I could not. I would just smile at them. Within seconds, their frowns turned into smiles and giggles. It worked every single time!"

Why is smiling so transformational?

- Smiling makes you feel good.

- Smiling makes you more attractive thanks to "emotional contagion." Humans are hard-wired to feel good when another person smiles because we perceive that person to be non-threatening. You know how it works when someone walks into a room with a big smile; they instantly lift the mood of everyone present! When you feel happy, the other person becomes more attractive to you. Smiling also makes you approachable, which can boost your social life. Smiling also conveys confidence, which is also attractive.

- Smiling creates rapport and trust, as your smile makes others feel good. When they feel good—when *you* make them feel good— they will be more inclined to like you, trust you, and help you. A genuine smile is a way to open doors to opportunity. Even on the phone, people can tell if you are smiling.

- Smiling enhances your health because it stimulates the production of feel-good hormones and suppresses the production of stress hormones which, if not released through physical action or meditation, can cause serious health problems.

- Smiling gives you better wrinkles. Let's face it, eventually we all get old and wrinkled. But wrinkles worn by decades of smiling and laughter are much nicer to look at than wrinkles worn by decades of frowning or sadness. As Mark Twain said, "Wrinkles should merely indicate where smiles have been."

According to behavioral scientists, babies and children smile about 400 times a day. The average adult smiles less than twenty times a day and people suffering from depression and anxiety smile less than five times a day (which makes the situation even worse). Sure, adults have responsibilities and worries, but adopting the habit of smiling more every day is a powerful attitude-changer that can make even the everyday "grind" seem better.

Make smiling more a natural part of your day. Make it a daily micro-habit.

1. Smile at yourself in the mirror.

Go stand in front of a mirror. Put a big smile on your face. It doesn't matter if the smile is forced. It doesn't matter how you are feeling. Look into your eyes and put the biggest smile on your face that you can manage. Within moments, even a fake social smile will transform into a genuine eye-crinkling smile!

Hold the smile for one minute. For an even more powerful effect, hold the smile for two minutes. Feel your mood becoming lighter with each second!

Smiling stimulates the release of serotonin, dopamine, and oxytocin. The more you smile, the better you feel—and the better you feel, the more you smile! What a wonderful upward spiral!

2. Practice gratitude.

If you truly feel that there is nothing to smile about, do your gratitude micro-habit first and then try smiling at yourself in the mirror. Gratitude primes you to have a more positive outlook that can help you see the good in every situation or person.

3. Be around people who smile a lot.

Let others activate the power of emotional contagion in your brain. Smile when they smile. And practice being the one who lights up a room with a smile. The more you do it, the better!

4. Practice!

It's sad that many adults have to practice smiling, but practicing smiling is a habit worth cultivating. Smile for just a few seconds every time you think about it: at work, when you are scared, when you are feeling shy, when you are tired, when you are upset, or when you lack confidence.

5. Meet the smile halfway, like Mona Lisa.

Practice holding a little Mona Lisa smile whenever you think of it. It's a half-smile, but it's one step closer to a real smile. You can instantly feel your face soften and relax when you do this!

Smile at the world, and it will smile back!

The Power Pose Habit

"Enthusiasm is the electricity of life. How do you get it? You act enthusiastic until you make it a habit." ~ Gordon Parks

The Power Pose is a micro-habit that boosts your confidence. In this way, it is a good primer for other habits, and it is a great motivator if you are having "one of those days" when motivating yourself to do even one simple thing can be a challenge.

The Power Pose is inspired by Leonardo Da Vinci's Vitruvian Man. This famous drawing supposedly depicts Da Vinci's concept of the ideal proportions of the human body. What is interesting is that the outward stance (feet slightly wider than the hips, arms outstretched upward and outward), actually causes a slight increase in testosterone levels in the body. Testosterone is present in both men and women, and one of its non-reproductive functions is to increase strength and confidence.

- Stand with your feet slightly wider than your hips.
- Stretch your arms up and outward, as if you were embracing the sky.
- Your chest is open and eyes are forward.
- Hold the power pose for about two minutes to positively influence your physiology.

Granted, two minutes are one minute more than the typical micro-habit, but this exercise can be priceless in preparing for an interview, a first date, a difficult talk with your partner, or any other challenge.

In the next chapters, you will discover ways to change your habits in specific areas of your life. You may find that some habits are easier to change than others, but once you get familiar with the process and start making a small change in one area, you will be encouraged to make changes in the more challenging areas.

It's *okay* to start easy! The whole point of starting small is to make it something so easy—so excuse-proof—that you will be empowered to expand on it as time goes on.

Creating new habits is extremely rewarding! You will find that it can be just as easy to move in the direction of your dreams as it is to stay where you are, or worse, move in the wrong direction.

Chapter 6: Habits for a Better Life

Activating the Snowball Effect

"Just do it! First you make your habits, then your habits make you!" ~ Lucas Remmerswaal

One positive habit can make a big difference. Imagine the impact of several positive habits across every area of your life. It's huge!

In this chapter, we will start a snowball effect of small habits that support positive change.

Placebo (Power of Positivity) Habits

"If you think a thing is impossible, you'll only make it impossible." ~ Bruce Lee

The placebo effect is most commonly used in medicine, but you can influence your mindset in any area of life by activating it.

Placebo is a Latin word that means, "I will please." The placebo effect is literally "mind over matter," and so it can be used anywhere—to achieve a goal, to become more energetic when you feel tired, to learn something complex, and so much more.

The opposite of the placebo effect is the nocebo effect ("I will not please"). We have discussed habits to help you stop worrying or focusing on what is bad or missing. But, since this is such a pervasive habit, it is worth repeating here with a slightly different angle.

Another way to look at this is positive thinking versus negative thinking. Many people mistake nocebo statements as reality when in fact, they are prophecies. When nocebo statements become your default way of thinking then your attitude, behaviors, and results will be very different from someone who practices placebo thinking.

Your mental habits determine your attitude, your attitude determines your behaviors, and your behaviors lead to (very predictable) results.

If you believe that an approach or treatment will work, the chances of it working increase significantly.

A placebo or a nocebo is a self-fulfilling prophecy based on your beliefs and expectations. It is what you tell yourself based on your knowledge of how things are, and your expectations of the future. For example, "It's hard to lose weight" is a nocebo statement that keeps you stuck. If you believe something is hard, you may not try. Another nocebo statement is "I am not good at remembering people's names." Instead of making an effort to remember names, you simply make the excuse that you can't remember.

The outcomes would be drastically different if you told yourself, "I enjoy exercise and eating healthy" or "It is easy to remember names."

If you are skeptical about the power of the placebo effect, consider this: Is it actually the physical application of pills or surgery that does the healing? Then how can healing using sugar pills be explained in dozens of studies on the placebo effect? Many studies have confirmed that in the vast majority of patients participating in them, spontaneous healing did not occur before the patient agreed that a proposed therapy would be effective; only once the patient was informed of a treatment that works did it heal them.

And again, the placebo/nocebo effect applies to every area of your life, especially when it becomes a habitual mental pattern.

If you believe that hard work and sacrifice are required for you to succeed, then that is what you will expect, and you will work ridiculously long hours. But if you believe that learning how to teach people to see your value is the way to succeed, then you will expect that, and once you showcase your value, success will naturally follow.

Your agreement that something will work is the key to activating the placebo effect. Likewise, your agreement that something will not work is the key to activating the nocebo effect.

Every single thought you have, regardless of what it's about, causes changes in the brain and a release of specific chemicals. That's right: your thoughts physically and functionally change your brain.

To see the nocebo effect in action, think about some negative phrases you may be using on a daily basis. For example:
- I'm so tired all the time! (Outcome: physical and mental fatigue)
- I'm too weak to lift that. (Outcome: learned helplessness and reliance on others)
- This drug is supposed to make me feel nauseous. (Outcome: nausea)
- I'm so stressed about money. (Outcome: anxiety)
- I'm terrible at remembering people's names. (Outcome: social awkwardness)
- I can't wake up without coffee! (Outcome: addiction to coffee)
- I can't do that anymore; I have a bad knee. (Outcome: regret from not even trying)

At first glance, these statements sound reasonable, like they are simply describing reality. But what would the outcome be if you changed the words you use habitually? What if you made a habit of putting a positive spin on what you say repeatedly?
- I have plenty of energy to do everything I need and want to do. (Outcome: abundant energy)
- I am learning the proper way to lift heavy things. (Outcome: physical strength and confidence)
- I am grateful that this drug is healing my condition and I feel better every day. (Outcome: relaxation, healing, and very likely, no nausea)

- I'm doing what I can to improve my work situation. (Outcome: noticing opportunities, and a positive attitude about your efforts)
- I like coming up with clever ways to remember names. (Outcome: confidence)
- I love waking up energized and ready to face the day! (Outcome: no reliance on stimulants)
- I am finding activities that I can do today. (Outcome: positive attitude, happiness)

The most important point is that placebos feel good, and nocebos feel bad. When you make it a habit to always look on the positive side of any situation, you will literally feel better (calmer, happier, and so forth).

Your words are very powerful. Get in the habit of using them wisely to boost your attitude.

Relationship Habits

"The world as we have created it is a process of our thinking. It cannot be changed without changing our thinking." ~ Albert Einstein

Habits can make you a better person, and by doing that, they improve all of your relationships. But before we get into habits that improve your relationships, there's one relationship that many of us have a few bad habits in. It is the most important relationship of all: the one you have with yourself.

Habit: I Love Myself

Throughout your life, you have adopted various unsupportive habits that eroded your natural self-love. Most of us do this, and we're very good at it. Self-love is the basis for making big changes. You make these changes because they are meaningful to you, they enrich you, they make you grow, they challenge you, and they make you overcome something you thought you couldn't.

Start each morning by looking at yourself in the mirror, smiling at yourself, and saying, "I love myself."

This little mantra, when repeated often, will create a subtle but powerful shift in your mind. If you enjoy doing nice things for people you love, you will give yourself permission to do nice things for yourself. That's motivation to make positive change.

When you love yourself, everything starts to fall into place! Repeat this mantra as often as you can throughout the day; when you do something good you are proud of, when you make a mistake, when you are faced with a difficult choice.

Overcoming the Inner Critic

Increasing your self-love is very important in boosting confidence, attracting better people, and putting yourself first (filling your cup so you can be there for others). Yet, it's something many people struggle with because self-love is often confused with narcissism, so we tend to put ourselves last when we should not, say yes when we should not, put ourselves down rather than appreciating ourselves...the list goes on!

One important habit to cultivate when it comes to self-love is to tame the inner critic; the inner voice that says, "I'm not good enough."

The inner critic constantly tells you that you can't do this, or that you don't have time/money/skills/connections, or that you'll probably fail, or that you are no good, or that you are not smart enough to get out of this mess you made for yourself.

Imagine you have a critic who followed you around all day and criticized everything you did. It's a terrible feeling, isn't it? But when you think a little deeper about it, this critical voice is just your brain trying to keep you safe! In essence, the brain loves to say, *"Don't do something new, it could be dangerous."*

Your inner critic is busy telling you what you can't do, but it does so with the intent of keeping you safe.

So, cultivate a habit of always replying in the positive to whatever the critic says. Here's how this works:
- The inner critic says, "You're not experienced enough to command a higher salary." You can reply with, "I'm very teachable, I learn quickly, I innovate, and I'm a great problem-solver. Companies always need that."
- The inner critic says, "You failed every time you tried that! Why bother trying again?" You can reply with,

"There's no such thing as failure, there are only lessons, and I have learned so much from these experiences!"
- The inner critic says, "You have never been lucky with money." You can reply with, "Luck has nothing to do with it. I've learned from my financial mistakes. I'm applying that knowledge and every day my finances are improving."
- The inner critic says, "Being fat runs in the family! You know this diet will fail!" You can reply with, "Actually, being inactive and eating junk food runs in the family! I love to move my body and eat healthy food, so it's easy to drop excess weight."

When you are your own inner friend who always sticks up for you, encourages you, supports you, and helps you see the best in yourself, you can always overcome the inner critic.

Cultivate this habit by always coming up with a supportive answer to the criticism. Focus on what you have, what you can do, and what you have learned.

Once self-love is evident in the way you talk to and about yourself and you have embodied habits that show self-love, your relationships with others will start to change for the better.

Positive Relationship Habits

Habits can have a powerful impact on your relationships. Any consistent and regular behavior will eventually become unconscious.

For example, let's look at John. John is a corporate manager with a large manufacturing team. Early in John's career, he had employees who were not doing their jobs, and he developed the habit of being condescending with them because he did not respect them. He didn't realize it, but this habit kept going when he was promoted and started overseeing a larger team. At this point, he does not realize he is talking down to his team members. He does not realize that he is universally disliked because he "mansplains" things to the women and constantly criticizes the men. John is completely oblivious to how his choice of words and his tone of voice affects his team's attitudes, and he wonders why the team does the bare minimum every day while other teams are driving innovation.

You can apply this concept to any relationship (romantic partnership, family, friends, colleagues, neighbors, etc.). For the sake of example, let's explore the impact of habits on romantic relationships.

Of course, there are wonderful relationship habits that many couples consistently do over the years, such as whoever gets up first makes coffee for the other or calling each other midday just to see how their day is going, always kissing each other goodnight, and always remembering special days.

The trouble arises when negative words and behaviors become habitual. Examples of negative relationship habits include:
- Not always showing respect or appreciation for your partner not just during disagreements but in casual conversation with your partner or publicly in social settings.
- Not taking the time to simply be together. Many couples get into routines where they are coexisting and doing things side-by-side, such as chores, activities with the kids, or automatically switching on the TV after dinner. Unfortunately, many couples rarely take the time to just be together, such as taking a leisurely walk together or spending an evening talking about random things.
- In today's age, many couples "retreat" to their phones and enter a different reality, engaging with people who are not present instead of interacting with the person who IS present.

The opposites of these habits are what most people consider the "work" it takes to maintain a happy and healthy relationship.

I put the word work in quotes because once these habits are adopted, they don't feel like work. They are automatic. Unconscious. *Easy*.

Imagine how these small positive habits will start to change your relationship:
- Saying something kind and respectful to and/or about your partner every day.

- Making time every day to simply be together with no agenda and no distractions.
- Putting the phone away during and after meals.

Adopting the right habits can change your relationship with your partner and also with your parents, children, siblings, and extended family members.

Think about some habits you have relating to your interactions with people that could apply to relationships you have at work and in your community.

Wealth Habits

"Winning is not a sometime thing; it's an all-time thing. You don't win once in a while, you don't do things right once in a while, you do them right all the time. Winning is a habit. Unfortunately, so is losing." ~ Vince Lombardi

Remember, a habit is something you do consistently and automatically. You don't have to make yourself do it, you just do it because it feels good and it's easy.

Delayed Gratification

Delaying gratification, or learning how to not seek pleasure through purchases, is a powerful way to help you get control of your finances.

When you want to purchase something, delay the gratification. Make yourself wait a full day before hitting the "buy now" button. This delay can be just enough for you to forget that you wanted this thing. If you still want it but don't need it, challenge yourself to wait another day, or even up to a week. This is a potent money-saving habit!

To quit smoking, let yourself have "cheat times," but put them progressively farther into the future. You never have to "quit" (which puts a lot of pressure on you). You only delay the pleasure until your next cheat time. You could start off with "in 30 minutes" and gradually work up to "tomorrow," and keep going. This way, the choice isn't between now and never, but now and later. This is much easier than the ultimatum of quitting.

Appreciation Without Possession

A friend tells the story of shifting out of a poverty mindset. He was in the habit of impulsively shopping just to ease his feelings of inadequacy; if his friends could afford a thing, so could he (whether this was true or not). This habit of not being careful with his money actually reinforced his expectation of never having enough money.

One day, my friend had a revelation. He saw something he liked, but this time, he truly could not buy it. His credit card was at its limit, and payday wasn't until next week. He stood in the store for some time admiring the object. After a while, feeling slightly dejected because he couldn't purchase it, he left. Very shortly afterward, something remarkable happened. He realized that he was fine. He didn't have a strong sense of longing to have this thing. He realized that he was actually happy without having purchased it (which would have gotten him even further in debt). He realized that the pleasure of seeing something and appreciating it was even better than actually owning it, because once he bought something, he felt guilty at having spent the money. He decided to try this again. That night as he browsed online stores, he decided to just enjoy the experience of looking. Once again, he reminded himself how awesome it was to see the thing, but not have to deal with the stress of owning it.

My friend got in the habit of seeing something online or in a store, soaking it in and appreciating it—then walking away. He quickly realized that he no longer felt poor. He had enjoyed the pleasure of a thing, but relieved himself of the shame and stress that inevitably came after purchasing something he did not need. Plus, he was getting control of his budget by not shopping.

You can do this too. Learn to window-shop (in person or online). Let yourself fully appreciate the idea of an object, but remind yourself that you do not need it and that your life will not be any richer for owning it. Let the experience of seeing and appreciating it be enough, just as you would appreciate a beautiful painting in a museum or a stunning natural view. This habit can save you a lot of money. It also helps you refocus on what is truly important in life: people and experiences, not things.

Habits of the Wealthy

Wealth habits—as practiced by many wealthy people—allow for wealth-building without struggle and without sacrifice. Habits aren't a get-rich-quick scheme, but they will build financial reserves steadily while allowing for money to fund fun. You won't feel like you are living on rice and beans for a wealthier "tomorrow," and you won't have to give up on living today.

- Wake up early, at the very least 3 hours before you begin your work-day. What can you accomplish during this time? Lots of small habits, which we'll get into in later chapters. These habits can very efficiently chip away at your wealth objectives, and you will also find more time for self-care, your relationship, and passion projects.

- Eat healthy and exercise. Your health truly is your greatest treasure. Choose healthy food to fuel your body and stay energized and healthy throughout the day with some form of exercise.

- Treat your time like money: think about how much time you waste on non-wealth-building activities that also don't contribute to your health, relationships, or passion projects and replace those time-wasters with habits that move you toward your objectives.

- Budget. Set a realistic budget and get into the habit of checking in with your budget once a week.

As you can see, it's little things like this—not "working harder," not working crazy long hours or playing the lottery—that will move you steadily toward your financial goals.

Raise Your Income Ceiling

We all have an income ceiling. Many of us want to earn more than what we currently earn, but we often believe that anything more than a certain percentage over our current earnings is impossible.

First, what is your current income limit? Imagine you were offered a job: you are qualified for it, it's your dream job, and the only question in the interview is, "What salary do you want?" That's right, you can choose your salary! Read through the list below and note the first statement that makes you feel uncomfortable:

- Your new salary is what you earn now, plus 25%
- Your new salary is what you earn now, plus 50%
- Your new salary is double what you earn now
- Your new salary is triple what you earn now
- Your new salary is 4x as much as you earn now
- Your new salary is 10x as much as you earn now
- Your new salary is 100x as much as you earn now
- Your new salary is as much as you want

The point at which you feel resistance and discomfort or have even a small thought like "that's unlikely," *that is your income limit.* That number is set in stone, unless you change your mental habits around an income ceiling.

The only reason you have an income ceiling is because you have been telling yourself that you have one, and what that amount is.

Your income limit has no basis in reality, it's just an arbitrary number that you believe to be true for you! Really! You can always acquire better skills and knowledge no matter where you are now. You can always make a career change that is better aligned with your strengths and talents, which could allow you to blossom into a coveted expert in a particular field.

Make a habit of raising your income ceiling by imagining yourself earning a salary you are slightly uncomfortable with. Every day, imagine seeing your bank statement with a fresh new deposit. Whatever that number is, be grateful for it.

A friend recalls a story where she was struggling financially as a freelance web designer. She was confident in her skills (her clients loved her!), but she was very shy in promoting herself because she had not been in the business for long. She thought she had to compete with people who asked for lower rates just because her portfolio was small. However, this modest rate was causing her intense stress because it wasn't enough to pay her bills.

When she started habitually thinking about making a certain salary each month, it felt very strange at first, like she was not worthy of it. However, one day, when that number started to feel comfortable, she spontaneously got on her freelancing platform and raised her rates by a small amount.

To her surprise, she started winning more bids. She quickly realized that her rates were tied to her perceived value!

After two years of slowly increasing her rates, one day she decided to double them and see what happened. She was absolutely shocked to see that now clients were seeking her out!

She attributed her bold move to double her rates to the mental habit of visualizing a certain amount of money coming into her bank account every month. Once that number became comfortable in her mind, she naturally took the steps to make it happen- not the other way around. In this way, her actions were not forced; she did not hesitate or second-guess herself. She did not worry about it. She did it because it felt right, and her results speak for themselves.

Every day, visualize your bank statement with a certain amount in it. It has to be a number that you are uncomfortable with, but one that you feel is attainable with effort. In other words, don't go from currently making $3,000 a month to visualizing yourself making $100,000. That will just create massive resistance in your mind. But bump your income up by a number that feels uncomfortable because you have never made that much, but it is an income that is in line with what your friends make (if they can do it, so can you). Repeat, repeat, and repeat until this number feels comfortable and then watch your actions follow this new mental pathway!

As you destroy one income ceiling, you can keep raising it, just for fun! Imagine all of the wonderful things you can do with your new income!

I Have More Than Enough

If money issues are causing you stress, here is a wonderful and simple habit to adopt. This habit is actually applicable to any area of your life whenever you feel you don't have enough of something. For example:
- You don't have enough money to pay the bills
- You don't have enough time to meet a deadline
- You don't have enough resources to achieve a goal
- You don't have enough skills or knowledge to get a better job
- You don't have enough friends to have a rich social life
- You don't have the health to enjoy life

This habit involves a simple practice of affirming, "I have more than enough."

If you are constantly telling yourself "I don't have enough," you are probably doing constant math in your head trying to figure out how you will get more of what you need, then you are constantly focused on lack. This leads to stress and unhappiness.

To dislodge this habit, the moment you start doing the math in your head, say to yourself, "I have more than enough." Remind yourself of what you do have in abundance. Do this as part of a gratitude practice. Let yourself feel the contentment, relaxation, relief, and security of having *more* than what you need.

Whatever "enough" means to you, imagine that you have it. And more.

I realize this may sound like a woo-woo approach to not having enough of something, but when you take away the need to do the mental math—when you relieve the stress—you activate what is called the Broaden and Build Theory (penned by Dr. Barbara Fredrickson) which states that when you feel happy and positive, you are more likely to take action, to innovate, and to explore alternatives. In other words, you open yourself up to avenues of getting more of what you need and, most importantly, these avenues would have been closed off to you in a stressed-out state.

Repeat this habit every single time you feel even a little bit of anxiety that you don't have enough of something. With practice you will become much more relaxed, and much more open to novel ways of getting what you need.

Health Habits

"If you always put limits on what you can do, physical or anything else, it'll spread over into the rest of your life." ~ Bruce Lee

Automating fitness is possible. When exercise becomes a habit as firmly ingrained into your daily routine as brushing your teeth, you will never have to convince yourself to go the gym. You will never have to battle the excuses. You will never look longingly at the couch, knowing that the temporary relief of choosing to relax will be offset by the disappointment of that choice.

Like any other habit, once fitness is automated, you will *want* to do it.

You already have the power of micro-habit health-oriented exercises on your side. Choose a micro-habit, or two at the very most, and do it for a month until you have established a habit of daily exercise.

If you can realistically devote five minutes every day to exercise, I invite you to do the following 30-Day Fitness Challenge. This challenge blurs the line between micro-habits and bigger habits.

Please note, it is always a good idea to talk to your doctor about starting a fitness routine and working with a fitness professional to make sure your technique is good (to prevent injury).

Give this fitness challenge 100% effort for 30 days (or until the behavior feels like it is part of your everyday routine). NO excuses are allowed. Treat this as a non-negotiable daily activity. Remember, you can hook this habit to an existing pleasurable habit, such as your morning coffee.

This challenge combines mental, emotional, and physical elements fueled by strong desire to look and, more importantly, *feel* better. Each of these are important for success, so again, make sure you do them all, every day, for 30 days straight.

1. **Affirm**: "I love moving my body and I am feeling stronger and more energized every day." You can repeat this as a mantra during your micro-habit exercises, each of which takes 30 seconds in the beginning.

2. **Engage**: Every day, do these nine movements for 30 seconds each. If this is too easy for you, just wait. By the time you are doing these movements for several minutes, you will have built a very solid fitness base and you can keep challenging yourself by adding more time as long as you don't skip a day.
   - Jumping jacks to warm up
   - Knee lifts
   - Squats
   - Wall sit
   - Lunges
   - Plank
   - Crunches or sit-ups
   - Pushups
   - Chair dips

3. **Reflect:** for 30 seconds, do gentle stretches while visualizing yourself as lean, fit, strong, etc. (whatever your health and fitness goals are).

And that's it! You can't overdo it when each movement only takes 30 seconds. Very shortly, these nine exercises plus gentle stretching will start to wake your body up, especially if you lead a fairly sedentary life.

Get in the habit of moving your body every single day for 30 days.

What happens after 30 days? If you found this challenging and you are content with this level, then stick with it. Give it another 30 days to further reinforce the habit, and then if you like, add 15 seconds to each movement.

If you found this sequence to be easy, add 15 seconds to each movement and the stretching session. You can keep adding to in 15 second increments each month if you like. By the time you are at six months, you will be doing each movement (and stretching) for a fairly significant amount of time.

- Month 1: 30 seconds per movement (total of 5 minutes)
- Month 2: 45 seconds per movement
- Month 3: 60 seconds (1 minute) per movement (total of 10 minutes)
- Month 4: 75 seconds per movement
- Month 5: 90 seconds (1.5 minutes) per movement (total of 15 minutes)
- Month 6: 105 seconds per movement
- Month 7: 120 seconds (2 minutes) per movement (total of 20 minutes)

The best part? This micro-burst of movements is concentrated, and you will start seeing measurable results very quickly.

After you've created a habit, you can keep adding time to the sequence as your time allows.

Exercise WILL improve the quality of your life. That is certain. What is not certain is how this new habit will affect other areas of your life.

Here are additional health habits that can help you get fit, lose weight, and sleep better:
- Eat a protein-rich breakfast, not sugary cereals, to fuel your day.
- Stay hydrated (many people are chronically dehydrated because the hunger signal and the thirst signal are almost the same, and people tend to reach for food first).
- Take an exercise break midday. Instead of fueling your afternoon with coffee and sugary snacks, take a brisk walk as part of your lunch break.
- Spend less time online and more time outside.
- Do strength training to build muscle mass that turns your body into a fat-burning machine.
- Walk every day. This low-impact exercise can be as intense or mellow as you want. The important thing is that you do it.
- Get out in nature as much as you can. Surrounding yourself with greenery lowers stress levels, according to scientists.
- Do flexibility and balance exercises to maintain agility and prevent injury.
- Do core exercises to support your lower back and prevent injury.
- Practice meditation or other mindfulness exercises to reduce stress.

Happiness Habits

"Happiness is a habit—cultivate it." ~ Elbert Hubbard

There is no one way to define happiness, because it is different for everyone. But there are a few things that make it hard to be consistently happy. Changing your thought habits in these areas is a game-changer!

The Habit of Anxiety

Anxiety is all too common these days. Most of us are overwhelmed with the fast pace of modern life and trying to juggle so many responsibilities.

Occasional anxiety about something big is normal. But if anxiety is chronic, it can paralyze you and prevent you from making decisions, and it definitely erodes your quality of life.

Anxiety is not a product of your circumstances as much as it is a product of your thought habits.

For example, anxiety around money is common for someone who repeatedly thinks:
- It's hard to make a good income because I don't have the education.
- I am only average. I don't deserve higher wages.
- I never have enough.

- The only way to increase income is to work more.
- It's hard to find a well-paying job.
- I am no good at managing my money.

Anxiety around money is rare in someone who repeatedly thinks:
- It's easy to increase my income.
- I am capable, clever, and resourceful.
- I always have enough.
- Somehow, opportunities just come to me when I need them.
- It's easy to live below my means and say no to frivolous spending.

To ease anxiety, imprint new thought habits around money.

What do you feel anxious about the most?
What is one reason why you aren't able to experience peace in that area?
What could you do right now if you felt calm and happy about that area?

The key is gratitude. Whether you have money or not, make gratitude a habit. Let's go back to the challenge of money, which is something that many people are anxious about. Every day, practice a wealth affirmation and add gratitude.

A wonderful gratitude habit is expressing gratitude for what you do have—something that brings you joy—every time you notice someone who has more than you.

It doesn't have to be a material thing! It could be:
- Time freedom
- A pet
- Great friends
- A supportive family
- A cozy home

Make it a habit to shift your focus from what is missing to what is beneficial about the situation. Not having financial abundance can teach you so much:
- Budgeting
- Living within your means
- Appreciating things without needing to own them
- How to better market your services

As with any habit, choose an affirmation and follow through with a gratitude practice. Put the process on repeat until you feel abundant. What happens next is that this new attitude of success will influence your behaviors. You will be more confident at job interviews. You will be bolder in taking opportunities. You will be smarter with your money.

The Habit of Complaining

"Feeling sorry for yourself, and your present condition, is not only a waste of energy but the worst habit you could possibly have." ~ Dale Carnegie

Complaining is a habit that erodes happiness. Most of us complain, at least a little. The problem arises when complaining becomes a habit. According to Robin Kowalski, PhD, from Clemson University, there are three types of complainers:

- The Venter: A person who is dissatisfied and is addicted to the feeling of dissatisfaction. They never want to hear a solution, no matter how brilliant and practical. They often reply, "Yes, but the problem is..." to every positive statement someone makes.

- The Sympathy Seeker: A person who always has it worse than everyone else and wants you to know it. Whatever your struggle is, theirs is infinitely worse. The Sympathy Seeker may not start a conversation with a complaint (like Venters and Chronic Complainers often do) but the moment someone shares a negative experience, they jump in with their own *massively bigger* tales of woe.

- The Chronic Complainer: Someone who ruminates about problems and dismisses potential solutions. They are so focused on the problem that they are completely closed off to the solution. All they see is that the door is locked, but they don't even notice the open window.

What's your complaining style? While it's okay to vent fears and frustrations, it needs to be done in a way that is focused on solutions, not on the problem. When complaining becomes a habit, you end up distressed most of the time.

Here's how to upgrade your complaining. Make it a habit to add a positive "but" statement to every complaint you make.

For example:
- The rain ruined our tennis game, *but we can go have lunch and see a movie instead.*
- My boss never listens to my ideas, *but I wrote down some ideas and emailed them to her so she knows I'm trying to solve the problem.*
- The traffic is horrible today, *but it gives us a chance to have a nice talk while we wait.*
- The pandemic made it hard to see friends and family, *but weekly family Zoom calls mean that my kids actually talk to their grandparents.*

If you are a venter, this will teach you to talk about potential solutions without keeping your mental and emotional energy stuck on the problem.

If you are a sympathy seeker, this will teach you to talk about what is good in your life, and what you are grateful for.

If you are a chronic complainer, this will teach you to focus on the positives and talk about what's good and what's working instead of what's going wrong.

When you upgrade your complaining habit, you still have an opportunity to vent your frustrations, but you aren't so focused on the negatives. This will instantly positively affect your attitude!

Confidence Habits

"There is no more miserable human being than one in whom nothing is habitual but indecision." ~ William James

Confidence is the attitude that leads to success in any area. Here you can develop a few habits that will help you overcome your fears and activate a very powerful internal motivating force.

Habit: Ride the Wave of Fear

Other than obvious physical threats, (we are talking about emotional fears here) we create our fears in the imagination.

Fear is not a thing that can hurt you. It is an emotion that comes from thinking about the worst possible outcome, and from giving emotional energy to that *potential* bad outcome.

The good news is that you control your imagination, which means you can imprint positive habits that empower and encourage you to act in spite of your fears.

This habit takes a little getting used to, but it is an extremely powerful way to soothe yourself whenever you feel afraid.

1. Whenever the feelings of fear come up, put all of your attention on the feelings you are having. You are perfectly safe in doing this; remember, fear cannot hurt you.
2. As you give ALL of your attention to the physical feelings you are having (and not to the thoughts that generated the fear) you will notice that the fear will subside within 90 seconds or less. What we feel as fear is just a chemical response to a thought, and if you don't feed the fear by focusing on the thought, the chemical response will dissipate.
3. As the feelings subside, say to yourself, "I can handle this."
4. Breathe deeply for a few moments and say to yourself, "I did it." Let yourself feel relief.
5. Imagine the *best possible outcome.*
6. If the fear arises again, repeat this exercise. You may need to do it several times.
7. Once again, allow the feeling of fear to arise, and shift all of your focus to those feelings. Just allow yourself to experience the fear. You are still completely safe.
8. As the feelings subside, say to yourself, "I can handle this."
9. Breathe deeply for a few moments and say to yourself, "I did it." Let yourself feel relief.
10. Imagine the best possible outcome.

What this habit does so powerfully:

- It allows you to experience the feelings of fear and be okay with feeling them! When you are comfortable *feeling* fear and managing it by shifting all of your focus onto the physical sensations, you calm down very quickly and take action. The fear did not hurt you. The only thing that "hurt" was the imagined possibility of something going wrong, and there is of course no guarantee that things will go the way you imagine them to go.

- It allows you to get unstuck from automatically thinking about the worst possible outcome. It allows you to give equal mental and emotional energy to an imagined outcome that is exactly what you want.

Courage is not physical bravery. Courage means letting yourself *feel* afraid, but taking action anyway.

Being able to ride the wave of fear is a powerful habit that can give you courage to face what you need to face, and since most of our fears in the modern age are emotional (i.e. fear of public speaking, fear of rejection, fear of failure, etc.), this small habit will empower you to overcome your fears and be more assertive.

Fear-Busting Habits

In addition to managing your emotions (or rather, feeling them without acting according to them), here are a couple powerful habits that will help you take action in spite of fear.

1. Break a large task or challenge into the smallest possible steps you can. You see, you don't have to take on huge challenges and act according to extremes. There is no way you

can climb a mountain in one giant leap. Just focus on the step you're about to take, and the next, and the next.

2. Practice positive "what if" statements. When we don't know what will happen, we default to imagining the worst-case scenarios. That doesn't feel great. It's what we do when we worry. Instead of always going down the negative "what if" road, practice deliberately asking positive "what if" questions. *What if it works out even better than I expect? What if she takes the news gracefully and we clear the air? What if nobody will be angry with me and instead, they understand my point of view? What if the treatment works and I kick this disease out of my body?*

The Galatea Effect

When faced with a goal or a challenge, many people will give themselves permission to quit by saying, "I'll try." Trying is not a commitment. It's a weak effort at best. But if you want to achieve the harder goals in life, not only do you need the support of small habits, you also need the support of the Galatea Effect.

The Galatea Effect states that if you believe you will succeed, you are more likely to succeed. This is a powerful internal motivator!

Don't give yourself permission to quit by saying, "I will try." Commit to doing, not trying. Create a habit of setting positive expectations of yourself:
- Expect that you will always give your best, and that the outcome is secondary to the quality of the effort.

- Expect that you are constantly learning and improving.
- Expect that every "failure" is really a valuable lesson that will help you in the future.

Chapter 7: Big Habits

Proven Ways to Adopt a Big, Bold Habit

"And once you understand that habits can change, you have the freedom and the responsibility to remake them." ~ Charles Duhigg

We have discussed a multitude of positive habits, and hopefully you are inspired to harness their immense power. You may already be having success adopting micro-habits, which is wonderful. In this chapter we will go deeper into how to adopt bigger habits.

I recommend you do not attempt this until you have mastered a few micro-habits. The reason is that creating a bigger habit can involve more work than you are used to at this stage. We do not want you to get frustrated by trying to change habits. The process should be easy and fun, so only start this chapter when you feel comfortable with your new micro-habits.

The only "rule" for this chapter is to change one habit at a time. Just one.

The Stages of Adopting a Big New Habit

"Let today be the day you give up who you've been for who you can become." ~ Hal Elrod

Creating big new habits is of course much more difficult than adopting small habits. However, if you have a strong "why" and you are committed to this big habit, here are the steps to take:

1. **Embrace the Why.** Build anticipation of what can happen as a result of the new habit. It's exciting, and you are "on fire" and eager to start. Be sure to build emotional energy around the reason you want to achieve this goal (because the goal, ultimately, is to make you *feel* something you aren't feeling now).

2. **Break it up but don't give up.** The biggest challenge comes when the "honeymoon phase" is over: regression to old habits, because they are easier. You can avoid the challenge of regression which often accompanies big goals. Tell yourself, yes, the new thing you are doing is difficult, it feels awkward, and you are not good at it. Remind yourself that you are a beginner at this new behavior, and that's okay! If this happens, you can simply break each action into micro-habits and gradually build on them to help yourself get through this beginner phase. Once the micro-habits take hold, you will find it easier to persevere.

3. **Gaining momentum.** The next stage, once you have a micro-habit in place and have started to build on it, is the breakthroughs when you are starting to experience results. Results may be small, but you notice them. This could be the ideal time to shift from micro-habits into slightly bigger habits, from walking for one minute to walking for 10 minutes for example,

and once *that* becomes a habit, move on to walking for 30 minutes. You know yourself. If you can move from a micro-habit to a consistent bigger habit (from one minute to 30 minutes) then do it, but expect to feel more resistance to a 30-minute walk than you would to a 10-minute walk.

4. **Relax and just do it.** Consolidation is the name for when the new habit is imprinted and it becomes your norm. You know a habit will "stick" when you find yourself doing it without any resistance. You just do it.

The Golden Rule of Positive Change

"The trick to success is to choose the right habit and bring just enough discipline to establish it." ~ Gary Keller and Jay Papasan

The Golden Rule of positive change is simply this: Break it down to what you *WILL* commit to on a daily basis. In other words, you don't have to adopt a big habit by making it a big habit.

Even big habits can be broken down into micro-habits that you can build on as you gain momentum.

Author Stephen King has a habit of writing 1,000 words a day, 365 days a year. Of course, that's his job, but that is a BIG habit for anyone for whom writing is not a profession.

But you can work up to a habit that is just as big, in smaller steps. How about 250 words a day (that's about how much text fits on the screen of your laptop)? On days spirit moves you, you could write 1,000 or more words. On days when it all feels overwhelming, 250 words is still progress. Even if you throw it out and rewrite it all later, your habit of daily writing will become your new normal within about 30 or so days—and then you could add 50 words at a time until you reach your goal of writing 1,000 words a day.

You see? Micro-habits mean no more excuses, no matter how big the ultimate habit.

Remind yourself of the analogy of climbing a mountain. If you look at the whole thing, it's HUGE and intimidating. So just lower your gaze a bit, look at the step in front of you, and take it. Then take the next one.

As time goes on, you naturally move from taking small steps to taking bigger and faster steps. But starting with big, fast steps almost always backfires.

A big habit will have massive results, there's no doubt. But don't set yourself back by taking on a huge habit. Let yourself start small and build on it.

Any habits, repeated hundreds or thousands of times over time, are not incidental. They become non-negotiable and they multiply.

Hooking a Habit to Another Habit

"Habit is the intersection of knowledge (what to do), skill (how to do), and desire (want to do)." ~ Stephen R. Covey

Making a new habit part of an existing habit can help you adopt bigger habits.

It's easiest, even with a micro-habit, to work on this at a time of day when you are less likely to be stressed or pulled in too many directions.

Identify one positive routine that's already in place during that time. For example, let's say you want to get in the habit of writing every day. If you do your best thinking very early in the morning, think about what you normally do during that time—for example, turning on the coffee maker. This habit already creates an atmosphere of pleasurable anticipation, and this makes it a perfect hook for a new habit.

When you turn on the coffee maker, open your computer or journal (whatever medium you are using to write). Don't write. Just get ready to write.

In this step all you are doing is initiating the behavior. For a week or so, do just this one step. This "hooks" the new habit to a positive existing habit because the positive feelings you have when turning on the coffee machine makes it easier to associate positive feelings with the new habit.

What is an existing positive habit that you could hook a new habit to? Once you condition yourself to start, you automatically create the desire to actually write (or go for a run, or read, or whatever the new habit involves).

One day, you will not give the new habit any more thought than you do when you turn on the coffee maker. You're already conditioned to start, which makes taking action so much easier.

You can use different hooks, too. Let's say you want to lose weight and you hook a habit of going for a brisk walk to your lunch routine. Instead of scrolling the internet after you finish eating, just put on shoes that you can walk fast in. For a week or so, repeat this—the moment you finish eating, put on your walking shoes. Don't even go for a walk yet. You can feel the anticipation starting to build as you do this, and when you are ready, start with a micro-habit: a one-minute walk. Remember, initiating the behavior will create anticipation and desire to complete the behavior.

Use the Right Language

"Life's battles don't always go to the stronger or faster man. But sooner or later, the man who wins is the man who thinks he can."
~ Walter D. Wintle

Since humans are language-driven, you could change the words you use to make a new habit feel more appealing. For example, if you want to establish a daily exercise routine, change how you talk about it. The word "exercise" implies hard work. The word "workout" feels like even more work (Who wants more work? Nobody I know!). Making the switch to "movement" or "play" makes it so much more pleasurable, and then you'll be more likely to do it until it becomes a habit.

"Movement," for example, is what you do anyway, even if you don't have your workout clothes on. Therefore, a fast walk with your dog counts as "exercise" (and it feels a lot more fun). Speed-cleaning your house, going dancing, a hike with a friend, a Brazilian dance class—all of these things are movement. If you attach more structured exercise to the idea of "daily movement," then you will have a different attitude about it. It becomes something you naturally do anyway, not something you are forcing yourself to do.

Track and Reward Your Progress

"If our mind remains freeze-framed by inhibiting and hampering habits, in an ever-changing world, we won't be able to get rid of that weird feeling of not belonging anywhere and not taking part in authentic life challenges."
~ Erik Pevernagie

We get a lot of pleasure from the neurochemical rewards of habitual behaviors. When you stay focused on your "why"—on the emotional reason you are adding this new habit—and when you track your progress, you can increase the emotional reward of the behavior as you are learning to make it a habit. Reward yourself with tangible rewards, too, to celebrate milestones and reinforce the positive new habits.

Challenge

Write down why you want to adopt a new habit. But this time, go beyond the feelings you will have once you achieve a goal. Think about how your life will have changed;

who will you become? What could your life look like in general, as a result of this new habit that allowed you to achieve a specific goal?

Give It a Test Drive

"If you do not pour water on your plant, what will happen? It will slowly wither and die. Our habits will also slowly wither and die away if we do not give them an opportunity to manifest. You need not fight to stop a habit. Just don't give it an opportunity to repeat itself." ~ Sri S. Satchidananda

I like the Test Drive approach because it takes all the pressure off adopting a new habit, especially when we are talking about a bigger habit. Only take this challenge on if you are confident you can stick with the new behavior for 10 minutes every single day for 30 days.

The rule is simple: Commit 10 minutes a day to doing something you love, every day for 30 days straight, with no excuses. After the end of the 30 days, take note of how this habit fits in with your daily life, how much resistance you are feeling to it, and most importantly, your results.

If the habit just isn't working out—if you are constantly forcing yourself to do it or finding excuses why you can't and you're not seeing results—then you have "test driven" this habit and found it did not work for you.

But *don't give up.*

Just change your approach.

First, make sure it's a habit that you really need (a habit that is aligned with your "why"). If not, then don't bother. Always take on habits that are meaningful to you, not to what you think you "should" do.

Second, if it is a meaningful habit and the problem is that you are simply up against a lot of resistance from a series of firmly-ingrained habits, you can chunk the habit down into a micro-habit and use the approach of incrementally increasing the time you devote to it. In other words, a 10-minute habit is a lot more challenging than a 1-minute habit.

Chapter 8: Putting It All Together

Creating an Amazing Life

"The soul grows into lovely habits as easily as into ugly ones, and the moment a life begins to blossom into beautiful words and deeds, that moment a new standard of conduct is established, and your eager neighbors look to you for a continuous manifestation of the good cheer, the sympathy, the ready wit, the comradeship, or the inspiration, you once showed yourself capable of. Bear figs for a season or two, and the world outside the orchard is very unwilling you should bear thistles." ~ Kate Douglas Wiggin

By now, you know how habits basically run your life on autopilot. You know how habits are made, and you have a collection of habits to choose from to elevate every part of your life.

In this chapter, I want to get into the power of the subconscious mind one more time to drive home the concept that your life experience really is run largely by your habits.

The Power of Your Subconscious Mind

"Busy your mind with the concepts of harmony, health, peace, and good will, and wonders will happen in your life." ~ Joseph Murphy

Here's a great example of just how powerful your subconscious mind is in automating your life:

Imagine you are driving down a familiar stretch of road. You are listening to music or lost in your own thoughts…suddenly, you realize that you have driven for quite some distance without being consciously engaged in the process of driving! This is a terrifying experience for many people when they think about all of the horrible things that could have occurred while they were mentally somewhere else. But, it's a common phenomenon.

During the drive, your conscious mind was focused on the music or your thoughts. But your subconscious mind had no trouble navigating the road, even switching lanes and negotiating turns, because those actions were *habit*. This would not happen on an unfamiliar road (with the exception of superhighways, which are all basically the same anyway). Operating a car is a habit. Driving familiar roads is a habit. Basically, your subconscious mind was in control of the wheel.

Most life changes fail. It's not for lack of trying, but because most people don't try to change their subconscious programming. Any time something becomes familiar and habitual, your subconscious mind is in control, not the conscious reasoning mind.

The secret to success in all areas of life is to change the mental habits, or the programming, that gives the subconscious mind direction. And this is HUGE. When 95% of your potential mind power is on your side instead of working against you, what could you accomplish?

Your subconscious mind doesn't argue. It dutifully does what has been programmed into it. If it is currently being run by outdated and unsupportive habits, then you will get unwanted results. There is really nothing woo-woo about this; just change the programming by introducing more positive mental habits and your behaviors and results will follow.

Dreams and goals originate in the conscious mind, but the subconscious mind is the engine, or the muscle if you will, to help you achieve them.

I'd like to share a story about Kristina. Kristina was overweight when I met her. She was very unhappy, she hated the way she looked, she had no confidence, she had no energy, and she had been on and off the diet roller coaster for her entire life. Whatever diet or exercise program she tried; she would have short-term successes. But inevitably, she would always revert back to her old habits, or worse.

I taught her about the power of the subconscious mind and how to create habits so she could automate fitness and weight loss.

Once she learned about the power of micro-habits as a way to reprogram her subconscious mind, she took the fitness challenge I outlined earlier (9 exercises plus stretching for 30 seconds per movement). By the time she had reached the 6-month mark, Kristina had lost about 30 pounds, which is not insignificant. She is now exercising 25 minutes every day and shows no signs of wanting to quit.

You can start the process of getting control of your subconscious mind right now. At night as you lie in bed, create a vision in your mind and mentally rehearse how you want to feel once your goal is accomplished. This will reinforce the micro-habits you have begun during the day.

Most people want results now. Willpower and discipline can get you to the finish line (achieving a specific goal), but all that work will be for nothing if it has not changed your subconscious mind.

Achieving goals actually requires far less work than what you are probably doing right now. And if you automate the work that is required, the *perception* of effort will be significantly smaller.

Achieving any goal is going to require far less effort than what you are doing now...unless of course you are not doing anything.

The key is, you have to be doing something, and you have to be doing it consistently until you aren't even aware you are doing it.

Wouldn't it be cool if you got up in the morning and automatically went for a run—just as automatically as when you brush your teeth, take a shower, get dressed, or put on your shoes? All of those habits that are automatic! You don't even think about them!

So, wouldn't it be nice to automate your fitness? How about your finances? Or nutrition? Once you choose the programming that goes into your subconscious mind—once you have imprinted positive, empowering mental habits—

then, and only then, will you have the proper mindset and you can automate success wherever you want more.

Again, since most people want results now, the key is to think of creating a habit as a result in itself. That's one piece of "code" that just got added to your inner operating system! That's one piece of information that will tell your mind what to focus on and what to hunt down!

Once you have your mindset right, your behaviors will automatically take care of themselves. If it's daily exercise you want, you won't have to think about it. If it's investing instead of spending, you won't have to think about it. If it's progress on a project, you won't have to think about it.

I like the analogy of flying as a way to illustrate the power of habits. The energy you put into getting the airplane off the ground is substantial, just like the energy you put into learning a new behavior, but once you're in the air, so to speak, you let your habit take over and take you out of your comfort zone into new realms of thinking and doing that move you in the direction you want to go.

New habits are the only way to overcome resistance to novelty. They are the only way to quickly regain homeostasis (optimal, balanced functioning) when you take on something new. In other words, the faster you create a habit out of a new behavior, the faster you will stop feeling resistance to doing this behavior, and the faster you will stop self-sabotaging yourself with rationalizations and excuses.

What is the story you tell yourself about money? Fitness? Love? What are the verbal expressions of what is imprinted (or programmed) into your subconscious mind?

The one thing you need to do to ensure success in any area of life is to tell a different story. In other words, imprint new mental habits.

New mental habits naturally and effortlessly lead to new behaviors and new results.

As you sow, you shall reap, and this really means that what you think about consistently—or habitually—is what will come about.

Therefore, investing in yourself by adding positive micro-habits to your routine can completely change your life's trajectory. At first, it might be just one percent. Over time, as the trajectories diverge and you add more good habits, the trajectories diverge even further. You move away from the old and toward the new—and it is effortless.

The reality is that the time is rarely just right to start something new, but you can always add a micro-habit to your daily routine.

You don't need massive breakthroughs. You just need small, consistent habits.

When Will You See Results?

"Great works are performed not by strength but by perseverance." ~ Samuel Johnson

You are probably wondering when it is all going to start to work. When will you start seeing the results of these habits?

The answer is: it depends.

Habits that are associated with the most challenging aspects of your life may yield results more slowly, because there are likely a great deal of unsupportive habits around that area that are still keeping you stuck.

For example, if your main challenge area relates to money, then adopting just one positive habit will not make a huge difference immediately because you likely have several other habits that go counter to that new habit. However, once you have one positive financial habit in place, it is easier to adopt another, and you will experience a gradual increase in momentum as each new habit chips away at your old ways of thinking and acting.

Don't give up! Each habit alone is small, but together they don't just add up, they multiply.

Here is a wonderful exercise you can do that will demonstrate just how powerful your mind is when you decide you are going to do something. It will help you see how attuned your brain becomes to hunting down your objective when you focus on a desired outcome and support it with daily habits.

The Blue Feather Exercise

"Success is the sum of small efforts repeated day in and day out." ~ Robert Collier

In his book *Illusions*, author Richard Bach suggests a creative visualization exercise that helps you guide your brain to focus on your goals—to give it the job of actively looking for something, whether you are consciously engaged in the "hunt" or not.

Visualize a blue feather. Imagine that you want this blue feather, very much. Don't worry about how or when it will appear in your life, just trust that it will.

Use your senses to paint a complete picture of this feather. Enjoy thinking about every aspect. Imagine its delicate weight. Feel its softness and marvel at the rich, deep blue color and the incredible design.

The habit comes in the form of thinking about a blue feather every day. Just enjoy the visualization. This simple 1-minute habit will yield results surprisingly quickly!

Within a very short time, a blue feather will manifest in your life in some way. It could be a real feather, a painting or illustration, part of a costume, a printed fabric, a stamp—however this feather appears to you, thank your brain for doing its job of seeking it out!

How does this work?

When you decide that you want something—that something is important to you—your brain becomes highly attuned to it. Just like when you decide you want a particular make and model of automobile, you suddenly start seeing it everywhere. Before you decided you wanted it, it was just part of the background; there, but not really in your awareness, and because you did not assign meaning and importance to it, you barely noticed it. Yet now, in some inexplicable way, it's *everywhere!* In reality, it was always there, but you didn't notice it simply because it was not important to you. Now that it is important, you become almost hyper-aware of it.

That is why, if you assign importance to a blue feather simply by giving it attention, it will appear in your life in some form.

Daily visualization of what you want—from the perspective of already having and enjoying it—is a habit that will prime your brain to be on the alert constantly, and to bring any clues, methods, or even the thing you want to your conscious attention.

That's right—you will not become attuned to just the thing itself, but the means to acquire it. All through a simple habit of daily visualization of what you want!

What You Can Expect

"Judge each day not by the fruit you reap, but by the seeds you sow." ~ Unknown

Once your habits have allowed you to achieve a significant goal, you will not be the same person you were when you started out on this journey.

You might notice:
1. You have a better quality of life
2. You feel more confident and your self-esteem is higher
3. You are happier and feel greater self-mastery

You will also notice that the goal was just a carrot, not the prize. The real prize is that you have become a person who could take a simple habit, repeat it, and add others, so that their effects became cumulatively stronger and exponentially more powerful.

Final Thoughts: Real People, Real Results

From Inspiration to Action

"Habit, not hope, is the last thing to go." ~ Pedro Cabiya

It is my intention that this book gave you the tools for creating meaningful and powerful habits that will literally automate success in any area of your life.

To recap, you will have the most powerful results if you stick to one or at the most two micro-habits every day until they are firmly established (always think of them as becoming as normal and effortless as brushing your teeth every day).

Daily consistency is vital. Your brain will be undergoing some changes with each new habit. Consistent repetition is key to ensuring that new neural connections become fast and efficient neural superhighways.

Real People, Real Habits

"What you habitually think largely determines what you will ultimately become." ~ Bruce Lee

Let's finish with some real stories of habits that real people have adopted. After all, most of the examples we are taught refer to celebrities and high achievers. But what about the "Average Joes" of the world, regular people who are making a difference in their lives thanks to new habits?

Here are some great examples of real people adopting positive habits and breaking bad habits. Notice the techniques that they used—techniques found in this book—and get inspired to make your own positive change!

- "I decided to become someone who eats healthy. I started adding one vegetable to each meal and reducing the amount of pasta and rice I normally eat. Once that felt normal, I reduced the pasta and rice and added another vegetable." ~ Douglas R.

- "I meditate for 15 minutes every day right after I brush my teeth." ~ Diane B.

- "When I moved to Madrid from Prague, I wanted to become fluent as fast as possible, but I didn't have a community of friends in Madrid yet. I decided to take a taxi to work and back every day, about a 10-minute drive. I made the habit of striking up a conversation with the taxi driver. These 10-minute conversations over the course of a year made all the difference." ~ Tomas V.

- "I broke my junk food habit by buying it, but then leaving it in my locked car. I live in New York. You can imagine how unappealing it was to go out to the car in winter. It worked! Even now whenever I think about junk food, I also think about chipping ice off the lock to get into my car after an ice storm. That association has completely cured my junk food cravings." ~ Raoul P.

- "I used to have a bad social media addiction. Yes, I was one of those people! I broke it pretty much instantly by logging out of the app every single time. What a pain to log back in, because I use one of those computer-generated passwords that's like twenty characters long." ~ Matt S.

- "I put my alarm clock in the bathroom so that every time the alarm would go off, I couldn't hit snooze. The only way to turn it off was to get up. Now, I just get up. I found that even if I'm still groggy I can wake up quickly by getting moving." ~ Kristina T.

- "My daughter would bite her nails constantly. I got her some nail clippers in a cute pouch and helped her clip them neatly instead of gnawing on them. It worked!" ~ Maria V.

- "I used to have the habit of late-night snacking. However, I got in the habit of brushing my teeth right after dinner. The minty taste is a trigger that signals 'I'm full' and I don't have the urge to snack before bedtime anymore." ~ Chris B.

- "I always lay my running clothes out the night before and put them right by my bed, which makes it easy to slip them on first thing and go run." ~ Laura M.

- "I used to just leave my clothes on the floor after I took them off. Then I moved the laundry basket closer. I put it next to my closet instead of having it in the laundry space." ~ Angela G.

- "I quit smoking by giving myself delayed 'cheat times.' I knew it was too much pressure on myself to 'quit' so I learned to wait until the designated cheat time. At first, I made it 10 minutes later. Then over time I worked up to an hour, then three hours, and before I knew it, I could wait until tomorrow. At that point I knew I was in control, not my addiction. I stopped for good about a month after training myself to wait until tomorrow." ~ Keith B.

- "I got rid of my junk food addiction by using the 'Free Beer Tomorrow' trick. I told myself, 'I'll treat myself to a McDonald's burger tomorrow.' Then tomorrow came, and I would say the same thing because 'tomorrow' means 'tomorrow' and not 'today' right? I admit it wasn't easy at first. But after a couple of days, I got in the habit of saying 'I can have that tomorrow' to any unhealthy food. I didn't know it could be this easy!" ~ Clare D.

- "I used to be a heavy smoker and then I got into weight-lifting. It was hard quitting smoking, though. I got in the habit of bringing a dumbbell with me on my smoke breaks. LOL, this was genius. I'd be standing there doing curls and hacking from smoking. After a little bit I'd just leave the cigarette in the pack and do the curls first. Sometimes I'd light up, but mostly I wouldn't. This totally got rid of the urge to smoke." ~ Pete M.

- "I used to drink around three beers every night. I started gaining weight because of this—your classic beer belly. Then I got in the habit of drinking a full glass of water before I would have a beer. This got me feeling bloated and I was able to cut down to two beers, and then one. Now I'm working on eliminating that one beer." ~ Sean M.

I hope that these real stories inspire you. None of these people are what you could call "high achievers" (at least, not the kinds of people whose names are well known). My approach is, if they can do it, so can I. And so can you.

It is so gratifying for me to see people making real changes in their life because of the ways I have shared to break bad habits and imprint new ones, and I sincerely hope that you will benefit from these methods.

I wish you the very best in your endeavors!

CPSIA information can be obtained
at www.ICGtesting.com
Printed in the USA
BVHW071427160223
658647BV00012B/687